Measuring Corporate Strategy

Measuring Corporate Strategy

CHARLES R. FERGUSON

DJ-I 1974

DOW JONES-IRWIN, INC. Homewood, Illinois 60430

First Printing, April 1974

Printed in the United States of America

Library of Congress Cataloging in Publication Data

Ferguson, Charles R 1925–
Measuring corporate strategy.

1. Management. 2. Management audit. I. Title.
HD38.F37 658.4 73-93361
ISBN 0-87094-072-4

Preface

"Unless," states Alvin Toffler in *Future Shock,* "man quickly learns to control the rate of change in his personal affairs as well as society at large, we are doomed to a massive adaptational breakdown." The concern that Toffler expresses for the future of mankind is a problem which also exists for managers of American businesses.

Executives are preoccupied with the phenomenon of our fast-paced technological development. They feel an urgent need to focus attention upon technology and techniques. Their concern with how to perform a business function effectively often overrides what should be their primary concern: whether or not the function should be performed at all, and, if so, how it relates to other functions.

During my 18 years of working with managers, I have been fascinated by the varying degrees of effectiveness they have achieved, ranging from poor to excellent. Without exception, I have found that those managers who are most effective think about and deal with the basic underlying concepts of their corporations.

The theme of this book is that an effective manager must be more concerned with concepts than with technology in the management of his company. The effective executive must deal with nothing less than the design of the corporation. Few corporations ever need a complete redesign, but all corporations periodically reach the point where some basic changes in design are essential to their survival. This book is based on the thesis that every corporation should stop, from time to time, to consider what these changes should be.

In these pages the process of examining and evaluating design concepts of the corporation is called a *concept audit.* The amount of change required by the concept audit will not be known, of course, until the audit is complete. Even if the change is minimal, the effort expended will not be wasted because the concept audit is also a learning experience in which management takes an objective look at the company in order to gain new and valuable insights into its operation.

ACKNOWLEDGMENTS

I would like first of all to acknowledge the influence of my clients on my thinking about management problems. The interaction that I have experienced with client managers has had a substantial effect in shaping my approach to performing the concept audit.

I would also like to acknowledge the important work of Kenneth Andrews of the Harvard Business School. His book, *The Concept of Corporate Strategy,* influenced the development of this book. The common ground of the two books is the premise that the shape of an organization should largely be molded by the strategies it is following.

Finally, I owe an expression of gratitude to Connie Stout who has so diligently typed and corrected the manuscript; to Nena Teed who made many suggestions for improvements in its organization and structure; to Robert Eichinger who contributed many valuable ideas; and to Melvin Bradford, whose assistance proved helpful throughout.

March 1974 CHARLES R. FERGUSON

Contents

1

The concept audit

The problems which most often plague corporate management occur at three separate levels of corporate existence. Before a reorganization is attempted or before the solution to any problem is accepted, an attempt should be made to determine whether matters have been studied at the proper level. The most recognizable problems occur at the operational level; they are caused by personnel who lack the facilities, skill, knowledge, motivation, or direction necessary to perform their tasks. Once the difficulty is understood, its solution becomes apparent and usually involves the performer—either his removal or some change in his performance.

Problems involving "techniques" occur at what may be called the technological level. At this level the basic problem is *how* a function may be performed efficiently: the solution involves the application of technology to a system or process that is basically sound and desirable. So far as top management is concerned, the solution to this class of problems consists of assigning someone with adequate technical knowledge or whatever other resources are needed to research or work out a satisfactory procedure. The technology involved may be difficult and the research expensive, but from the perspective of top management the solution is quite straightforward.

Many corporate problems, however, lie deeply imbedded in the most fundamental level of corporate existence: the *basic conceptual design* of the company. Problems at this level may appear to be caused by managerial ineptitude or by technically imperfect systems. Yet no amount of replacing and reshuffling personnel at the operational level, nor any degree of additional technical sophistication, will succeed in these cases. The causes of such problems are more basic and lie in erroneous assumptions as to whether or not a process should be performed, what its real purposes are, and how it is related to other elements of the corporation.

Such problems are the direct responsibility of top management, and their solutions call for changes in the conceptual design of the corporation. This is no small task. Examining conceptual design is the most fundamental way in which to view a corporation and, at the same time, the broadest and most complex. The conceptual design of the *total* corporation includes *all* of its elements: organizational structure, management methods, economic characteristics, physical configuration, environment, information flow, and decision-making systems.

A well-designed corporate conceptual framework provides the basis around which detailed and technical systems may be built. This framework must be very sound if the systems are to be sound. The framework also produces designs of organization structure, systems, facilities, and management which are complementary to each other in carrying out the work of the corporation. Because the conceptual framework is so basic to an effectively operating corporation, it seems obvious that managers should give careful attention to reexamining their company's conceptual design *before* shifting personnel and *before* installing advanced technology. That they do not is evident from the frequent instances of efforts to increase the efficiency of functions that should not have existed in the first place: programs to train managers in skills they will never need, and compensation plans paying for executive qualities that have no value to the corporation.

The conceptual design of the corporation, its appraisal, and its redesign require an intimate understanding of the corporation in its environment. Developing a corporate design is essentially "designing in" a means of executing corporate strategies and "designing out" those concepts which do not support strategies in force. This is a job for top management, not technical specialists. Managers need an effective means of appraising the quality of the corporate conceptual design with which they are concerned. The concept audit is a procedure that can aid them. The initial step in conducting the concept audit is to identify factors critical to the success of the company.

FACTORS CRITICAL TO SUCCESS

Each company has its own set of critical factors which must be satisfied if the company is to achieve success. These factors are situations, internal or external to the company, which require the special attention of top management, if not the chief executive. For example, a company may require highly specialized management, well grounded in its particular technology. If managers of this caliber are scarce, the company must take steps to insure that it retains its resident management talent. It must train junior managers in order to replenish, when necessary, the top management resource pool. When managerial talent is an important factor to a company's success, its degree of criticality rises in direct proportion to the availability of the required management resources.

Within any given company, a multitude of such factors must be dealt with if the company is to succeed, or perhaps even survive. For the purpose of the concept audit, however, the critical factors are only those situations requiring a special effort on the part of top management. To know a company intimately is to know its critical factors. Most chief executives are aware of their company's critical factors although they may never have written them down or verbally communicated them. Often the chief executive is aware of them to such a degree that he fails to communicate their criticality to his managers because he assumes that they are generally understood.

If a manager is new to a company or if he wishes to reassure himself that he knows his company's critical factors, he can develop a check list such as the following:

1. What are the objectives and goals of the corporation?
2. What are the significant advantages over competition which must be achieved or maintained?
3. What are the competition's advantages which must be prevented, overcome, neutralized, or counteracted?
4. What corporate strengths must be developed, protected, or utilized?

5. What corporate weaknesses must be avoided or overcome?
6. What features give the corporation important uniqueness or character?
7. What activities or processes of the corporation require special attention of top management?
8. What is the particular niche or function of the corporation in its market?
9. What important trends are occurring in the corporation's market or technology?
10. What are the opportunities upon which the corporation intends to capitalize?

Once the critical factors have been identified, strategies for handling them can be examined. This examination goes to the roots of the corporation, to its basic conceptual design.

In the final analysis, a critical factor is whatever the chief executive says is critical; he identifies factors within the corporation that must be taken care of by developing the proper strategy and by developing the proper conceptual design for the execution of the strategy.

STRATEGY–BASIS FOR CONCEPTUAL DESIGN

The most logical basis for the appraisal of corporate conceptual design is the question, "What exactly is the design supposed to accomplish?" One of the most effective ways to begin is to consider conceptual design as a *means of carrying out corporate strategy*. Too often, strategy is considered to be merely a mental activity or attitude whereby top management adopts a stance or direction concerning a general plan of action. It is more productive, however, to take strategy out of the strictly mental realm and absorb it into the corporate design. There is no specific guideline or principle as to what the strategies of a particular company ought to be and the development of corporate strategies is, itself, a difficult and complex task. Strategies are derived from those circumstances and conditions which have special significance to the company's ability to meet its goals and are referred to collectively under the heading "critical factors."

Strategy is a compressed statement of the general scheme required for taking care of a critical factor. Strategies must be distinguished from goals, which are more properly defined as critical factors. For example, a company may have the goal of increasing its sales by

10 percent over the next year. The strategy for meeting this goal may be to open a new territory, introduce a new product, or find new opportunities within customer companies. If cost reduction is a goal, then strategy is the general method by which a reduction in cost can be achieved. For example, some U.S. companies are adopting the strategy of reducing costs by having their products assembled across the border in Mexico. An alternative strategy may be to build an automated plant. Still a third strategy may be to install a cost reduction program in the present plant. A fourth strategy may be to redesign the product; and yet a fifth may be to reorganize the plant management structure. In fact all of these strategies, in one form or another, might be adopted simultaneously.

To understand conceptual design, "concepts" must be distinguished from value judgments, and "conceptual design" must be distinguished from systems design. For example, the manager who is developing the conceptual design for a compensation system may make the value judgment that young managers should not receive salary increases at a rate exceeding 10 percent a year. This theory may be based on a value judgment that larger increases will make the young manager too demanding in future years, and that a bonus or salary increase in excess of this amount will not buy management anything in the way of additional motivation. This theory may or may not be correct; the point is that in designing the concept of a compensation system the value judgment may be built into the conceptual design. The actual conceptual design of the compensation system, however, will be far more encompassing than the value judgment. The concept design, then, is directly related to the job to be done rather than to some general principle of organization design or manager motivation, or some general practice of management style.

System design is the detailed fleshing out of a concept. The concept is top management's idea of how they want a strategy executed. The system is the specialist's detailed design of the concept. The system design takes into account all of the mechanical and technical factors required to make the concept work.

System design is carried out by the technical expert. Top management is responsible for the development of strategies for meeting critical factors and conceptual design for carrying out the strategies. Conceptual design guides the technical experts in designing a system. However, it is much broader than the system.

PREPARATION FOR THE CONCEPT AUDIT

The preparation for a corporate concept audit is a sequence of three steps:

1. Reviewing the company's situation and environment in order to pinpoint factors critical to its success.
2. Defining existing strategies or creating new strategies required by the critical factors.
3. Deciding in what general areas supporting conceptual designs may be required for each strategy.

This series of steps is illustrated, for a typical company, on the following chart. Four general conceptual areas are designated: managerial, which includes concepts concerning the types of managers who will be needed, how they will be obtained or developed, and how they will be managed or motivated; organization structure, including concepts concerning how activities will be directed, controlled, and coordinated, and how particular talents and skills will be brought to bear on the activities of the company; management of resources, related to allocating critical resources to the most productive uses; and finally, the total corporation including its systems and decision-making processes.

Critical factors are only briefly suggested on this chart—manager, product or service characteristics, raw material, etc.—with no discussion of the reason for their criticality.

As shown on the chart, one or more strategies may be articulated for each critical factor. Each strategy can, in turn, be embodied in more than one conceptual area or design.

Let us follow through a series of steps on the chart, taking the subject of management. The chart shows that providing for an adequate number of highly qualified managers in the future is considered a priority sufficiently critical to require special attention. Two strategies for satisfying this critical need are indicated, including finding and bringing in experienced managers from the outside and developing managers from young recruits through the company's own internal development program.

If the latter strategy is adopted, its conceptual implementation may take place in several areas. For example, the organization structure can be designed to provide beneficial risk-taking experience for promising young managers. The compensation system can be de-

		Conceptual Area			
Critical Factors	*Typical Strategies*	*Management Structure*	*Organization Structure*	*Management of Resources*	*Corporate Systems and Decision Making*
1. Management	Source of: Secure from outside	x			
	Develop and train	x	x	x	
	Performance of: Manage for motivation	x	x	x	
2. Product or service characteristics	Create internal skills to produce	x	x	x	x
	Develop a means to stay in constant touch with market	x	x		x
3. Raw material	Control the source	x		x	
	Create internal skills to produce	x	x	x	x
4. Physical facility	Continuous change of design to meet demand market		x	x	x
	Types of production: Long run-standardized	x	x	x	x
	Custom	x	x	x	x
5. Control of operations	Control direction or level of effort	x	x	x	
	Coordinate groups or functions	x	x		x
	Control performance	x	x	x	x
	Utilize special skills	x	x	x	
6. Technological skills	Bring in from outside	x			
	Develop internally	x	x		x
7. Financial resources and financial stability	Reallocate resources as needs change			x	
	Control resource productivity	x	x	x	x
8. Marketing	Posture: Market to an industry		x	x	x
	Market a product or service		x	x	x
	Continuously detect market opportunities	x	x		x
	Utilize manufacturing capacity fully		x	x	x
9. Distribution system	Posture: Maximize service or market contact		x	x	x
	Minimize cost or investment in inventory		x	x	x
10. Corporate skills	Posture: Make policy only at corporate level	x	x		x
	Provide staff service at corporate level	x	x		x
11. Company reputation and prestige	Develop advertising and public relations	x	x		x
	Achieve deserving performance	x	x	x	x

signed to attract, reward, and motivate high-performing managers. A performance evaluation system can be designed to distinguish among managers according to their level of performance. In making a concept audit, each critical factor is worked through to see that all related strategies are being adequately supported by conceptual designs.

A concept audit should not be confined, however, to only those concepts related to explicitly stated strategy. By taking a more comprehensive approach and examining all major areas of corporate conceptual design, the audit may uncover numerous important areas that can be improved. It may in fact discover additional implied strategies, and thereby make it possible for these to be evaluated. The comprehensive approach to the concept audit involves a questioning and challenging of the state of conceptual development in the corporation. The following questions illustrate the nature of this analysis:

1. Is there a general understanding of the economic concepts operating within the company, including the behavior of costs, the derivation of profits, and the flow of assets?
2. What are the important systems of the company, and are they recognized and treated as systems?
3. What is the operative level of understanding concerning the trends and development of the company, and to what degree is it translated into specific plans and strategies?
4. What are the critical resources of the company, and what conceptual basis is used to improve their productivity?
5. What kind of climate exists to support management vitality within the company, and what kind is needed?
6. What specific things are intended to be accomplished by and through the organization structure?
7. What specific things are intended to be accomplished by and through the compensation system?
8. What are the typical approaches taken to improve the functioning of the corporation?
9. What changes have been identified as being needed in the design of the corporation?

By a careful examination of strategy and by the analysis of questions such as those on this list, the manager becomes familiar with the nature and purpose of all the important conceptual areas within his company. He is then well prepared to conduct a concept audit.

THE CONCEPT AUDIT

Performing a concept audit involves taking inventory of existing corporate design concepts and assessing their appropriateness for carrying out the strategy and other important functions of the corporation. The concept audit leads to the revision and improvement of conceptual design and, therefore, forms the basis for planning a corporate reorganization. Before discussing the audit procedure and objectives, it will be helpful to explore the idea of concepts a little further and to examine the forms in which they exist in corporate design.

Within any particular functional area, there are usually several types of concepts which vary according to their susceptibility to redesign. The most flexible are "system" concepts which describe the deliberately designed systems, programs, structures, formats, and configurations of the corporation. Usually these concepts have been documented and are, therefore, quite visible and accessible to the audit. It is necessary in defining system concepts to distinguish between the conceptual framework involved and the more technical and detailed systems design or implementation. "System" concepts are defined by describing the following:

1. What is the purpose or end result to be achieved?
2. What constraints or compromises are involved in achieving the desired result (including any tendencies for suboptimization)?
3. What are the essential or basic processes involved?
4. What is the nature of the inputs and their transformation, and what outputs may be predicted from given inputs?
5. What units of the corporation are involved, and what are their particular roles or responsibilities for the end result sought, as well as their relationship to all other units involved in the concept?

Once the "system" concepts have been identified and understood, they can be redesigned and incorporated into the overall reshaping of the corporation—that is, if they do not adequately support its strategy.

Another type of concept can be expressed in the form of a model. Such concepts or models are expressions of the behavior of specific elements of the corporation under given conditions. If sufficiently developed, they make it possible to predict the output or results of specific happenings or inputs. They may describe economic and cost behavior, a production process, or other elements of the corporation. "Model" concepts are important to the concept audit because they increase management's understanding and, therefore, its control over the operation of the corporation. The phenomena represented by model concepts may or may not be susceptible to direct attempts at redesign. For example, an economic model may explain the inherent relationships between operating costs, rate of activity, profit generation, and cash flow—a system that was not "designed" itself because it is the indirect result of the design of all of the other elements of the corporation. It simply describes what exists. Because such a pattern is the indirect result of other elements, it is susceptible in varying degree to redesign.

Finally, there are "attitudinal" concepts which exist solely in the minds of decision-making executives. A manager's opinions and modes of thinking can exert a consistent influence on his decision making completely independent of corporate policy or design. Attitudinal concepts are especially important in the concept audit because they have a large impact on the operations of the company but may be completely hidden. This is especially true if the basis of the concept is in the manager's unconscious. A relatively common example occurs in executives who operate under concepts (attitudes) that prevent them from developing a successor because they unconsciously fear strong subordinates. Other attitudinal concepts may have been inferentially transmitted to the executive, as policy, from a higher level of management, or perhaps inherited from his predecessor. Attitudinal concepts are thus not necessarily derived from personal philosophy or attitude. In any case, once attitudinal concepts have been identified it is appropriate to ask whether they should be taken out of the realm of the strictly mental and incorporated more firmly into some conceptual design. To be realistic, attitudinal concepts may not be subject to control since they may require changing the basic attitudes of individual managers. The concept audit should aim as a minimum, however, to identify the major attitudinal concepts at work within the corporation.

WHAT KIND OF INFORMATION IS REVEALED BY THE CONCEPT AUDIT?

A concept audit is conducted by taking an inventory of existing concepts and evaluating their collective ability to carry out corporate strategy. The audit seeks to answer the basic question, "Is there a conceptual design in the structure for carrying out each important strategy, and if there is, does it do the job?" In the process of answering this question some very interesting and useful information may be uncovered.

First, it is often discovered that top management has a concept it thinks is in operation but which has never been actually implemented. The executives responsible for administering the function in question are operating under an entirely different concept:

> The management of a small manufacturing company became concerned because it had failed to meet its growth and profit objectives for several years in a row. After a painstaking analysis, the manager concluded that there were no basic faults in the company or its personnel but that key personnel were, for some reason he could not understand, not fully committed to the goals he had set. He then decided to adopt a program of management by objectives as a solution. Very little improvement occurred as a result of the program until the manager realized that although he thought he was adopting a concept whereby managers established their own goals, in reality his subordinates still regarded the goals as those of the top manager. His concept was not in operation because they were merely going through the mechanics of management by objectives to satisfy him.

Perhaps even worse is the function without *any* conceptual basis:

> One sales manager, who uses a charismatic approach to management, strives for expanding sales volume by concentrating on inspiring his salesmen to increase sales by working harder and longer. Plans of action based on concepts derived from an understanding of customer needs and attitudes or competitor weaknesses which could increase the effectiveness of his inspirational approach are almost never developed by him. His continued effectiveness is directly related to his level of energy and his inspirational skills.

What degree of effectiveness will be achieved by the sales force when this charismatic sales manager suddenly moves to another company? On what conceptual basis will the sales force operate? Hopefully the next sales manager will develop a plan of action and communicate it to the sales force.

The existence of a highly structured routine or procedure does not necessarily indicate that a conceptual design is in existence. Sometimes a manager will apply a faulty conceptual basis for carrying out a strategy:

> A manager stated that one conceptual basis for his organization structure and information reporting system was to hold managers individually responsible for their performance. An analysis of his company revealed, however, that the real facts were otherwise. There was no clear-cut way to associate results with individual executives and in no real sense could they be held accountable for results.

The manager must, therefore, test the validity of his conceptual assumptions. Evaluation of conceptual validity sometimes leads to a completely different yet valid and "results-producing" conceptual understanding:

> A manufacturer of refinery equipment felt that in order to reach its goals for its share of a market it had to adopt a strategy of dealing more with the design engineers and less with purchasing agents of its major oil company customers. The method used in attempting to carry out this strategy was quite simply to be more aggressive in making direct contact with the engineers and to get to know them better. Instead of improving the company's position, it worsened it by alienating both the purchasing agents and the engineers. The strategy was made to work by creating a highly specialized engineering and research group inside the company which could aid the customer design engineers in refinery design. The customer engineers recognized the value of the specialized design assistance they were able to get and requested assistance from the company's personnel providing the contact needed at a critical stage in the competition for individual jobs.

Many procedures and systems are developed in aimless fashion with no clear idea as to the real purpose to be served by the system. This happens frequently when technicians apply their skills without adequate conceptual guidance.

The concept audit uncovers certain important strategies which have no conceptual basis within the corporate design. It is possible, of course, to adopt strategies without design support. The question is whether a mental attitude is enough.

Finally, there will be important functions which have escaped the attention of management but which nevertheless are operating on some conceptual basis. The basis may have been carried over from some previous time or it simply may have evolved out of unrecalled circumstances. Such concepts, perhaps never having been articulated, may be defined only by inference from what is actually going on. Under such conditions of development, they are not likely to be supportive of strategy and, indeed, may even be in opposition to strategy. It is therefore extremely important that they be discovered.

The concept audit reveals, in clear and distilled form, top management's ideas of how a corporation ought to function. The audit makes these ideas available for comparison among management personnel and brings into view any major differences that may exist. Recognition of these differences can be quite significant in working out plans for reorganization.

It should be obvious from this discussion that the concept audit is concerned not only with managerial concepts to be "designed into" the structure, but also with whether or not the concepts are understood by managers at all levels and, most importantly, with whether or not the concepts are really operational in the day-to-day functions of the company.

HOW TO CONDUCT A CONCEPT AUDIT

There are important reasons why the concept audit should be looked upon as a self-evaluation process and performed by a task force of the corporation's own high-level managers. First of all, it is a major step in strategy implementation. Next, it is a large and painstaking job which may take too long to accomplish unless the work is divided among several teams. Furthermore, participation in a concept audit is a learning experience which cannot be paralleled either in daily activities or in formal training programs. The special quality of the concept audit as learning experience comes from two sources: (1) it provides practice in conceptual thinking which all managers need; and (2) it exposes the participants to the design concepts under which the company is operating, affording special insights into how the company functions. The name suggested for this task force is the Strategy Implementation Task Force (SITF).

Many companies, in assigning a task force to perform the audit, encounter a shortage of managers with the ability to think conceptually. At least one member (preferably the team leader) must be adept at conceptual thinking. If there are not enough conceptual thinkers inside the company, they must be supplemented by outsiders.

Before the concept audit begins, all members of the task force must be instructed on the procedural steps of the audit and its purpose. This includes a thorough presentation of the critical factors and strategies which have been developed. Also, since managers typically do not deal with concepts as such, a discussion of conceptual thinking is required. They need to know how to distinguish between a conceptual and technical design, how to identify operational concepts, how to describe concepts, and how to find means of matching strategies with operational concepts.

The first task of the team in performing the audit is to prepare an inventory of all existing concepts. The initial step in accomplishing this task is to interview the executive who has policy-making responsibility over the area being examined and ask him to articulate the concepts he believes are operating or should be operating there. He may not have detailed knowledge of the operating concepts, but he will normally be able to state accurately the basic intent or purpose of most of them in the areas for which he is responsible. This, of course, is a good starting point for the team.

The next person who should be interviewed is the manager responsible for administering the conceptual design. He is most likely to understand the actual conceptual basis of the operation. It is important to compare their two points of view and to pinpoint significant differences. This alone may make the conduct of the concept audit worthwhile.

The most fruitful way to uncover concepts is to ask the right types of questions. These will vary depending upon the conceptual area being examined; but the following questions are good examples of how to begin the development of concepts.

Organization structure

How much structure is appropriate for this organization?

Which functions need to be coordinated?—What means should be used to achieve coordination?

Is the structure designed to make real accountability possible?

Is the decision-making process designed so that the quality of decisions can be improved?

What organizational relationship should be established between subfunctions?

Has the organization been designed to make the most effective use of the talents available?

Management

What corporate strategies are dependent upon management style and management qualities?

How well are management capabilities matched with position requirements?

Is the need for conceptualizing skill recognized adequately at each management level?

Are experience specifications stated in terms of time or in terms of meaningful exposure?

What basic manager attitudes are required for key positions?

What management style will create the attitudes and produce the performance critical to this company?

How democratic should the organization be?

How should managers communicate with employees regarding performance?

Are individual managers' goals aptly tied in with corporate goals?

Are performance reviews fully utilized for developmental and motivational purposes?

Management compensation

What are the overall goals of the compensation plan?

What corporate strategies should the compensation plan support?

What values are established by the compensation plan?

How generous should fringe benefits be?

What problems are caused by omission of a pension plan?

Are stock options necessary?

What kind of managers does the company wish to attract?

Is compensation properly used as a response to performance?

Should response to performance be related to results or to the manager's performance and development?

Resource allocation and management

Do managers manage operations instead of resources?

Are managers willing to eliminate inefficient resource users?

What resources limit the corporation's ability to achieve goals?

Has the productivity of all resource users been identified?

Has direct profit contribution been established for each profit source?

Is resource velocity maximized?
How much information on profit contribution and resource productivity is needed?

The total corporation

What is the corporate posture toward social forces at work in its environment?
Is the corporation keeping up with the development of knowledge?
Have major corporation-wide systems been identified and dealt with as systems?
What is the nature of changes the corporation should make?

After the concept audit team has developed its answer to these questions, it is necessary to examine the answers very carefully and apply a test of reality to them by collecting actual facts from records, documentation such as charts and diagrams, and observations of actual operations. By examining the decisions that have been made, as well as employee attitudes, they must *infer* the underlying concepts that are actually being followed. In short, the team must look at tangible effects and determine their cause conceptually.

At this point in the concept audit, concepts have been identified and analyzed as to whether or not they are actually in effect and whether or not they are appropriate. The audit has also revealed where concepts are needed but do not exist. The concept audit has, therefore, provided a basis for the detailed evaluation of the design of the corporation. This basis includes:

- Identification of specific areas of the corporate design which need to be improved.
- Identification of strategies or critical factors which require the development of new concepts.
- Identification of areas in which appropriate concepts exist but have not been made operational.

In addition, the concept audit will have revealed to the top manager the overall state of development of conceptual thinking in his company. He may now judge how extensively and how well the conceptual basis for his company has been developed. He will also be able to evaluate the ability of his executives to deal with concepts and to decide if further developmental activities would be appropriate. The completed concept audit may also be used to inform the members of the Board of Directors about the basic functioning of the company. It should provide them with new insights into its nature and aid them in making the important decisions.

The implementation program in which concepts are revised or developed, translated into detailed designs, and actually implemented may now take place. The concept audit team members are well qualified to participate in this planning because of the superior insights into the corporation's conceptual design which they have developed during the audit.

The work of developing and implementing new concepts may very well involve all aspects of the company–managers, allocation of resources, structure and systems–since the concept audit deals with all of these. This can be a very large job requiring a period of several years to implement fully and it should be carefully planned in order that it be a manageable task. One important step in the implementation program is the careful presentation of old and new concepts to the management group. This is the most effective means of preparing them for the changes to come, since the exercise reveals the logic of what is being done.

CONCLUSION

This chapter has defined the basic requirements of and the approach to be taken in conducting the concept audit. The remaining chapters apply the approach to major areas common to all corporations. For the purpose of consistency, the group of people conducting the audit have been referred to throughout the book as the Strategy Implementation Task Force (SITF) although they might just as well be described as the audit or project team.

The task of the SITF is lengthy as well as all-encompassing and, therefore, it is necessary that they obtain an overview of the elements of the audit at its inception. The most logical place to begin is with the basic structure of the organization.

2

Concept audit of the organization structure

The starting point of the work for the Strategy Implementation Task Force (SITF) ought to be the organization structure. Although structure seldom gets the blame or credit for corporate success that it deserves, its sound design is necessary to successful implementation of many important strategies. In fact, almost every corporate strategy can be executed or supported through the design concepts embodied in the organization's structure.

There are several major areas of conceptual design in which the organization structure provides a particularly effective means of executing strategy. One of these is in controlling behavior patterns of managers. The organization structure may be regarded as an instrument which replaces or supplements the efforts of the manager in directing the accomplishment of the corporate mission. It can actually take over part of his function of directing, motivating, and controlling behavior. Further, if properly designed, it can do this as well or even better than the executive could personally, thereby saving his time for other more important tasks. The organization structure can be designed to aid in maximizing the utilization of human resources. To an important degree the personnel involved in the corporation should influence the design of the structure. Finally, the design of the organization structure affords numerous opportunities to support functional strategies. These functional strategies involve the corporation's posture toward its market, its competitors, and its general environment. Through conscious consideration of the functional implications of the design of its structure, it may determine how to maintain its most effective relationship with its market, how to maintain a competitive edge, or how to capitalize on its strengths. Each of these areas offers strategy-executing opportunities and should be examined carefully during the concept audit.

On the other hand, organization structure can include design concepts which do not support already adopted strategies or the structure can permit the existence of personal power and influence which operate in opposition to a chosen strategy. In the beginning of this work, the overall conceptual areas of organization structure should be examined and evaluated by the SITF. Specific concept audit questions concerning these areas are covered in this chapter.

Questions about organization structure

What behavior should be defined by the organization structure?

What behavior is taking place outside of or in contradiction to the organization structure?

Does the organization structure define how individual units are related to each other?

Does the structure define how individual units are related to the overall mission of the corporation?

Is the definition of the organization structure sufficiently complete to reduce the need for direction from top management to a minimum?

Do managers make a disciplined effort to act according to the organization structure?

Is it necessary for managers to act in contradiction to the organization structure in order to be effective?

Does the organization structure cause tension among managers?

A very general concept which will help the SITF establish the right frame of mind for conducting the concept audit of organization structure is to think of structure as *a means of defining and controlling organizational behavior.* This concept is appropriate for the corporation as a whole as well as for individuals.

By specifying the arrangement of functions, the division of responsibilities, and the interaction between units, the structure makes it possible for diverse elements to act as an integrated whole. It assures the performance of important functions by specifying in what manner and by whom they will be performed. Structure establishes direction and priorities by placing functions and responsibilities at the appropriate organizational level. Guidance and direction for individual executives are provided by position definitions, whether or not they are in writing and whether they are vague or specific. This guidance, provided by the structure, does not take the place of motivation or inspiration normally provided by good leadership or incentive plans. It does, however, support motivational efforts and is always helpful in directing even the most willing and inspired of managers. When operating within a framework of a logical organizational structure, a great deal of the manager's time is freed from instructing subordinates and he is able to spend more time in inspiring higher levels of commitment to achievement. On the other hand, structure can directly influence the motivational level of executives by the degree to which it restricts their freedom to operate within the organization. As structure becomes more and more defined, its effect begins to change from being directive to being restrictive.

In evaluating structural concepts the SITF should recognize that although structure is an important means of specifying behavior, it does not automatically control that behavior. Discipline is required to assure that activities take place within the framework of the structure. Making individual behavior conform to the pattern prescribed by structure requires conscious effort from managers. The SITF should, therefore, examine actual behavior patterns to determine if they are different from what is specified by the organization structure and, if so, why. It is possible for an organization to have a well-thought-out formal structure and yet perform poorly because of important, but unnoticed, deviations from that structure. On the other hand, the existence of a poorly designed structure need not be fatal. The executive whose responsibility is improperly prescribed may recognize a more workable arrangement and adapt his actions to an informal but more effective arrangement outside the putative structure. It is also possible for an organization to make a poorly designed structure work simply by being determined to make it work. An organization governed by an illogical structure can still accomplish its mission through sheer willpower, although it will usually be able to do so only at the expense of great energy and not without causing an unusual amount of tension.

For example, a medium-sized manufacturing company was engaged in the manufacturing and distribution of food products. For its size, this company had an unusually complex set of operating conditions that required very close coordination of all of its major functions—marketing, purchasing, finance, and manufacturing. Some of the major problems that had to be faced on a regular basis were:

> Raw materials were mostly agricultural products such as sugar, cocoa, and almonds that had to be secured from all over the world. With the wide price fluctuations which normally occur in these markets, the company often had to change its source for those materials and often went so far in reacting to price fluctuations as to change the product recipe. Some 3,000 different recipes had to be scheduled through this production facility. Scheduling was made more difficult by the seasonal characteristics of the business. Over 60 percent of the company's annual sales volume occurred over a four-month period. In order to make the most efficient use of its production facility the company made annual forecasts, scheduled an almost constant level of production, and kept off-season production in cold storage warehouses. Marketing was nationwide, directly to retail outlets and by its own salesmen who were paid salary plus commission. Thus, it was for several reasons very important to maintain a close tie between marketing and other departments. The marketing group had the only input available as to market trends affecting the company's somewhat flexible product design, and of course it was on the basis of forecasts from marketing that vast quantities of products were produced ahead of demand and stored. Finally, the marketing group needed to react at various times to what was in storage in order to move what had not been moving as originally forecast. The seasonal nature of the business required outside financing. And the financial executive also had to be very closely tied in with operations to make sure that sufficient funds were available and that finance costs were held to a minimum. The organization structure of this company had a major flaw in that too many executives reported directly to the President. These included two regional marketing supervisors, the purchasing agent, the quality control manager who was in charge of product design (recipes), a manager of production scheduling and inventory control, the controller, and a production manager. Because of the large amount of coordination necessary among these executives, the President typically worked about 60 hours per week performing that function—that is, he spent his time primarily in seeing that one unit communicated adequately with another and that each unit responded properly to the rest. In addition to this effort, individual

executives, being conscientious, initiated meetings with other executives so as to work out common problems and frequently developed and installed new paperwork systems to aid in controlling the flow of work through the organization. This company was moderately successful *in spite of* an organization structure that did not support the company's objectives. It was successful because the executives wanted it to be successful. They spent the extra effort and endured the strains of continuous crises. However, their efforts could have been much more effective if the executives had been grouped in a more logical fashion, one which would have allowed for much of the coordination the President could not accomplish. A number of alternatives could have been found if they had taken the time to think about them.

Almost any structure will work if the manager wants to make it work badly enough; however, because structure can play such an important role in supporting the manager's direction of the organization, the SITF should be especially diligent in evaluating concepts related to organizational behavior.

How much structure?

How much structure is appropriate for this organization?

What circumstances in this company indicate the need for an increase rather than a decrease in structure: fixed assets, internal efficiency, technology, managerial preference, the need to fix the response to events which may occur?

Before answering this question, the SITF needs to make sure it understands which strategies should be implemented. Some strategies favor more, and some favor less, structure. A popular trend of thinking holds that structure itself is bad and that, as a matter of principle, it should be held to a minimum. This is based upon the philosophy that employees and managers deserve the opportunity to work in a manner that is self-fulfilling and that requires a high degree of self-determination. Regardless of how one feels about structure, it should be obvious to any corporate officer that there is considerably more at stake than "fulfillment" of managers and employees.

The pressure for more structure increases in direct proportion to the degree of "fixedness" of the company's assets. A company which has a large portion of its worth in fixed assets such as plant and equipment will naturally adopt strategies that involve a lesser degree of organizational freedom than companies whose assets are more liquid and, thus, more flexible. Because of the unchangeable nature of the assets, a "fixed asset" company must do everything it can to assure that the course it is bound to follow involves the least possible risk. All efforts to provide this insurance inevitably lead to a more structured organization. At the opposite extreme is the company whose primary assets are the talents of its personnel, as in a firm of professional people such as lawyers or doctors. The peripheral work of accounting, record keeping, and office management in such firms may be highly structured, but the key work of practicing medicine or law is completely unstructured insofar as the manner in which each individual carries out his professional activities is concerned.

A common (but not universal) strategy leading to a high degree of structure is the emphasis on internal efficiency. For some companies, low production costs are essential to success. No one would argue that internal efficiency is not an imperative requirement in mass production industry. And, at least to date, no one has been able to demonstrate that the level of internal efficiency which mass production requires can be achieved without a high degree of structure specifying precisely who does what and in what manner. A high degree of structure is also required by companies depending upon any sort of advanced technology, which demands rigidly prescribed procedures and thus prohibits individual freedom.

In highly developed technology, conditions occurring in the production process are usually predictable and the correct procedural response is foreknown and well defined. This is, in fact, the definition of technology. Any company which is dependent upon it must have a structure which supports it. When a company is not critically tied to a technology or to the priority of internal efficiency, a high degree of structure is seldom necessary. In such companies excessive structure may even be detrimental to the initiative and general satisfaction of employees. Where initiative and innovation are highly critical, as in professional firms, the SITF will quickly see that concepts of design involving less structure are most appropriate, even at the expense of internal efficiency.

Usually, when a manager states that he prefers an unstructured environment, he is referring to the organizational level at which he operates and not to the level he controls. The SITF should recognize, however, that this arrangement may be quite appropriate for that situation.

The manager of marketing for a manufacturer of industrial equipment managed his department in a highly structured way. He required his salesmen to prepare detailed sales forecasts of sales by product by territory. He further required the preparation of weekly itineraries in which the salesmen's routes and prospect names were planned in the most precise manner. Sales materials were carefully planned to support the salesmen's presentations, which themselves were carefully organized by the marketing staff. Each salesman carried a pricing and policy manual which carefully spelled out the company's policies and the answers to many questions which the salesmen might run into. In short, the marketing manager structured his department so that it operated in the manner he desired and also that, once organized, it required a minimum of his time for routine affairs. The manager himself, however, had almost no fixed pattern of operating. He spent enough time in routine checking to assure himself that operations were being carried out according to his wishes but mostly he looked for the situations where he could make the most productive use of his time—which might lead him into almost any area. He might decide, for example, that one territory was not measuring up to its full potential and spend his time in that territory trying to diagnose the problem. Or he might reach the conclusion that the overall marketing strategy could be sharpened up and conduct a market research study to gain further insight into the attitudes of customers and potential customers. The basic management philosophy of this manager, in short, was that routine operations ought to be highly structured so as to free his time for the more critical problem areas.

When the manager increases the degree of structure in the organization under him, the organization is bound by that structure. It has less freedom in its response to events, and it makes fewer demands on the manager's time. The manager himself, therefore, has more freedom if he chooses to spend the released time in paying attention to the organization's outside environment. And the net result may be greater rather than reduced responsiveness to the environment.

Finally, the task force needs to recognize that the amount of structure in an organization may not be purposefully related to strategy at all. There is a natural tendency in all organizations to move toward an increased degree of structure. This tendency springs from the manager's desire to reduce the uncertainty with which he must deal. The tendency operates continuously so that the older a company is, the more structured it becomes unless there is a conscious effort to negate this trend. The level of structure required in an organization is that degree of structure necessary in order to answer affirmatively these four basic questions:

1. Is the structure designed to achieve the necessary amount of coordination among functions, departments, subdepartments, and activities of human resources?
2. Is the structure designed so that functions, departments, subdepartments, and individuals are accountable for results?
3. Is the structure designed to execute all important functional strategies?
4. Is the structure designed so that the organization can make optimum use of its human resources?

Satisfaction in these four basic conceptual areas represents the core purpose of organization structure. The SITF must therefore carefully examine these areas in its audit of the organization structure.

Coordination

What are the special needs for coordination?
What means should be used to achieve coordination?
Which departments have a special need to cooperate?
Which departments have opportunities for conflict?
Which functions need to be coordinated? What means should be used to achieve coordination?

The concept audit includes a careful examination of interrelationships among functions so as to identify specific requirements for coordination. Some of these requirements are indicated directly by strategy. For example, the execution of strategy to make the manufacturing function fully responsive to the requirements of individual customers strongly indicates the need for a specific conceptual approach designed to coordinate manufacturing operations with marketing. Other needs for coordination are only indirectly related to a particular strategy and may be identified by searching for functions which have special needs for interconnection. The SITF should therefore look for those conditions requiring coordination in a special search, as well as throughout the audit process. The following list will be helpful in directing the SITF to discover these conditions:

- A series of activities which are in different departments but are interdependent in accomplishing a common result. The processes of receiving, producing, and shipping a customer order are an example.

- –A function or department which must respond quickly to demands for service from a remote source.
- –Groups of departments which depend upon the same technology and therefore require adherence to the same procedures and techniques.
- –Conflicting personalities or special spheres of influence where lack of coordination may impede the normal progress of operations.
- –Departments which compete for the company's resources but operate without specific decision rules for achieving appropriate compromises in case of conflict.
- –Departments which interact regularly on matters in which their respective roles are not always completely defined.
- –Departments whose interrelationships for any reason tend to cause stresses and strains among the participants.
- –Situations requiring continuity of attention across departments.

Aside from situations represented by a step-by-step process, there are special conditions which may change in unpredictable ways, and these should be monitored, or coordinated, in order that the appropriate corporate unit may respond to such change. For example, a bank may feel that an appropriate strategy is to pay close attention to the status of individual customers in order to serve them as their financial needs change. This would require some means of coordinating each customer's activities as opposed to allowing a customer to deal independently with various departments of the bank. Other examples of areas requiring continuous attention are the utilization of a facility, the conduct of a research program, the solving of a problem, the flow of balance sheet items, or the development and introduction of new products.

After identifying the situations requiring coordination, the SITF is ready to evaluate the means by which it is being achieved.

Actually, it is possible to achieve coordination by means other than organizational structure–for example, by designing a *system* for the flow of communications. Coordination by "system" is possible only in a situation that is highly predictable. Where practical, it may be preferable to accomplish coordination through systems concepts rather than concepts involving "structure," since less executive effort is required. The need for coordination may sometimes be eliminated by merely clarifying the relationship between two functions. This is often the case when the need for coordination is indicated by confusion or bickering between two operating units.

The most common, and positive, concept for achieving coordination through organization structure is to do so directly by placing the units involved under the same manager. Indirect approaches include the concept of a staff coordinator, classic examples being the product manager and the project manager. Such "managers" usually have responsibilities for coordinating activities in all of the line departments related to the specific product or project. Another indirect approach includes the concept of designing two separate departments so that they have corresponding subdepartments, and giving them direct access to each other. For example, both the marketing department and the production department could be subdivided by product line, in which case coordination would take place spontaneously between the respective subdepartments unless there were inhibiting factors present.

The SITF will find that some needs for coordination conflict with others. Departments cannot be divided, for example, to assign a single individual direct responsibility for coordinating the activities of all production operations, and, at the same time, to provide for a direct chain of command for coordinating the activities on a specific product line or project. These responsibilities cut across the organization structure in different dimensions and a decision has to be made to establish coordination over one dimension directly and over the other indirectly. In evaluating operative concepts of coordination, the SITF should consider which dimension requires the strongest and most positive coordination and designate it as the dimension to be coordinated directly. In considering the appropriateness of employing a structural concept to achieve indirect coordination, the SITF should recognize that a staff coordinator is imposed on an organization structure for the purpose of influencing the line managers. This, in itself, may cause an additional strain on the organization by introducing conflicting interests. There may be a conflict in interests between the staff coordinator and the line manager since their performances are measured in different dimensions, or there may be a conflict among several staff coordinators who are striving to influence the line manager to different ends. In evaluating the concept of achieving indirect coordination by placing corresponding units of different departments side by side, the SITF needs to ascertain whether the need for coordination can be fulfilled at this level by what amounts to cooperation, or whether it must take place at a higher level.

Accountability

Is the structure designed to make real accountability possible?

Can results be traced to specific individuals?

Do managers have sufficient authority to influence the results for which they are accountable?

Requiring accountability of managers at all levels is a strategy which, when properly executed, can make a fundamental difference in a corporation's ability to meet its goals. In evaluating the concepts underlying accountability, the SITF must examine the attitudes of managers as well as the design of the organization structure.

Accountability is the organizationally imposed control that ties individual behavior to results and therefore is considerably more significant than the mere designation of who shall report to whom. It can exist only if there is a mutual understanding between the manager and his subordinates that successful performance in a specified area is a requirement for job security. When accountability exists, the subordinates expect to be called upon *individually* to answer for results and, if results are inadequate or lacking, they expect to be replaced after some reasonable time. Individual managers achieve this atmosphere of understanding in accordance with their own particular management style. Some may use the power of their positions or personalities to create a threatening atmosphere that arouses fear. Other, more mature, managers take a less personal approach and let it be understood that the very health and vitality of the organization require accountability. The price for failure to require accountability is paid in poor results and impaired effectiveness of all managers, both good and bad. Where accountability is not required, managers who are not inclined to perform well are not inspired to change, while managers who do perform well are demoralized.

Although the achievement of real accountability requires a philosophical commitment to the concept, structure must be designed properly in order to make real accountability possible. Organizational arrangements that make it impossible to require accountability of individuals are found frequently in both large and small organizations. Accountability is largely a question of how responsibilities are assigned. And yet, at the same time, a reasonable theory of accountability assumes that these assignments must be both divided and grouped properly. Accountability requires that the results for which a manager is held responsible be uniquely identified and associated with him. Ideally the manager's area of responsibility should be solely his, with no overlapping with those of other managers. This would be the case, for example, with the head of an autonomous division. Shared responsibilities dilute the effects of accountability, although it must be admitted that the spirit of cooperation which may be generated can offset this disadvantage. It must also be admitted that the ideal division of responsibility is often not possible because of other organizational factors. For example, a group of departments responsible for a series of functions all leading to the same end result must share the responsibility for that result.

Fortunately, there are many opportunities for strengthening accountability by making responsibility for results more clear-cut. This can obviously be accomplished whenever individuals perform the same function in a common pool. Their output should not be intermingled, but should be kept separate and identified with the responsible individual. Sometimes all that is required to accomplish this is a system of record keeping. Often, however, it may be more effective to make a distinction between different classes of work and assign the classes to different individuals.

On the other side of the coin, it is just as essential to *combine* functions properly as it is to separate them. In order to hold a manager accountable for results, it is widely recognized that he must also be given a proper measure of authority. A proper measure of authority includes control and decision-making power over all of the functions essential to the results for which he is held accountable.

Ideally, the collection of functions under each executive is such that they form a self-contained unit receiving input and producing output independently of other units. In practice very few units can operate with this much independence; but independent units should be striven for because the greater the degree of interdependence, the greater the sacrifice of accountability at a given level. Accountability for intermediate objectives is obviously better than no accountability at all. However, organizations should be designed so that accountability is required for ultimate results wherever possible.

Following through in the evaluation of the concept of accountability will lead the SITF to another very interesting concept of executive management methods: actually only top managers in highly centralized organizations have permanent accountability. The manager at the top of a highly centralized organization may or may not realize that only *he* is accountable for ultimate results. The character of the job of managing is drastically different for the executive over managers whose individual responsibility is a fragment of those results. In the latter case, the top manager must devote a considerable amount of attention to coordination. The work of coordination is essentially the task of bridging a gap between two functions and is not essential to the extent that the gap need not exist or could be placed lower in the organization. Also, it is the nature of the work of coordination to be dealing with the elements of the *work itself.* The coordinating manager is immersed in the actual work going on and is directly involved in carrying it out by acting as an intermediary among the units. His orientation is to the work itself. The manager who has divided the work under him so that he can hold individual managers responsible for segments of the results has an orientation toward the managers themselves. He is not less concerned with or less accountable for the ultimate results, but his essential relationship is with the managers rather than with the work itself. His involvement with the actual work is generally indirect as he is managing the managers and not the work. Consider, for example, a general manager who has both a marketing manager and a production manager reporting to him. If he is involved in the coordination of the work he will be dealing with questions of communication and response between his two managers. If, on the other hand, coordination is achieved largely by other means such as systems design or organizational arrangements then the general manager is free to spend more time specifying and reviewing performance with the managers. Aside from any other considerations, this is his most productive effort because of the leverage it provides for his own energies and talents.

Committees and accountability

Is the decision-making process designed so that the quality of decisions made can be improved?

Have committees been designed into the decision-making process appropriately?

Are there committees making decisions that should be made by individuals who, unlike groups, can be held accountable for results?

"Management by consensus" and decision making by committee are in conflict with the strategy of requiring individual accountability. There are certain decisions, however, which are appropriately made by committee. These can be easily identified by the SITF. They include decisions in the following situations:

–When the possible consequences of a decision are so great they might affect the well being of the company, the combined judgment of a knowledgeable committee may be best. Decisions involving large capital expenditures or setting a new major corporate direction fall in this category. Such decisions become irreversible when set in motion and at that point accountability becomes pointless.

–When decisions are critically related to the interests of a component internal group rather than the objectives of the organization as a whole, it is proper for these decisions to be made by that group.

–When the character of decisions is such that their results cannot be known until after a very long period, it may be impossible to hold the decision maker accountable. Indeed, he may be gone by the time the results are in. This is the type of decision involved, for example, in offering a new type of life insurance policy.

What is missing for the individual manager in group decisions is the opportunity to make his own mistakes. Managers learn as much, perhaps more, from their incorrect decisions as from their correct ones. The impact of being solely responsible for a bad decision is a very lasting one. It may be argued with some validity that the expectation of being held personally accountable for their decisions will cause some managers to make decisions that involve as little risk to themselves as possible. The SITF may evaluate this possibility by examining the manner in which accountability is defined. If it is defined well, it will include a requirement for innovation and risk taking. Under such conditions, the excessively cautious will be identified and corrective action taken. It is through the observation of performance that the company learns to improve its total decision-making process. By holding individual managers rather than committees accountable, the company can make a systematic effort to improve continually the quality of its decision making.

Functional strategies

What organizational relationship should be established between production and marketing?

What subfunctions within marketing and production require special organizational placement in order to receive appropriate emphasis or attention?

What are the most critical needs for coordination among the subfunctions in marketing and production?

To what is the company committed to marketing?

What is the company's basic approach to marketing?

To what basic type of production process is the company committed?

What production characteristics are significant in their influence on the marketing function?

Certain corporate strategies are specifically related to how major functions such as marketing, production, or finance will be carried out. The SITF should focus on these functions, individually, to assess how well the organization structure is designed to execute the strategies involved.

To relate these questions to functional strategy is a task requiring careful analytical work on the part of the SITF. Each company will have its own answer which can be revealed only by insights into the logic of a particular function within a particular company. The audit should begin by examining the most basic strategies. In marketing this usually involves what the company is committed to marketing and its primary marketing approach. A company's marketing commitment is to whatever is central to its marketing effort, which will not change unless the company makes a major change in direction. A chain of supermarkets, for example, is committed to its distribution system consisting of buyers, warehouses, trucks, and supermarkets. The merchandise it handles may change considerably through the years, depending upon how it perceives its market; but its entire marketing effort is designed around making full use of its outlets for distribution. Some of the more common marketing commitment strategies are commitments to:

Product or product line.
Technology or capabilities.
Serving an industry.
Operating a distribution system.
Capitalizing on a possessed resource.
Satisfying a particular need.
Capitalizing on access to a market.

The marketing approach strategy indicates what management believes to be the most effective marketing technique for that particular company. For example, approach strategies include:

Persuasion.
Problem solving.
Perception of needs.
Logistical efficiency.
Establishing a unique price, quality, or geographic position in the market.
Specialization based on an in-depth understanding of the market.

The SITF may find that more than one strategy from each of these lists, as well as other types of marketing strategy, apply to their particular company. By developing an in-depth understanding of these strategies, and then searching for appropriate means to carry out their execution, the SITF will find themselves developing a logical basis upon which to evaluate design concepts operating in the situation under review.

Table A illustrates a number of hypothetical but typical instances of design concepts related to strategy. For example, the first set of basic strategies is for a tobacco company producing and selling cigarettes. The company is committed to this product and sells it by outward communication (advertising) without any particular reference to consumer needs. It *has* the product, and its marketing task is to find ways to convince the largest possible portion of the potential market to buy the product. From this strategy it follows that persuasion and advertising are highly critical and that control over advertising must be recognized and provided for in the design of the organization structure. In fact, all the activities involved in marketing

TABLE A
Typical marketing strategy and organization design concepts

Basic marketing strategies			*Organization structure design concepts*
Commitment to	*Example*	*Primary marketing approach*	
Product	Cigarettes	Persuasion	Advertising and the development of sales techniques are important functions and should be placed at a high level in the organization until they are functioning well. The distribution system, including selling and access to the market, are important and need to be highly structured and controlled. The sales organization should be organized along product lines.
Technology or special capability	Specialized steels	Problem solving	The problem-solving ability is a skill which needs to be protected by training or by research and should have an important position in the organization. The problem solvers need close support from engineering or research facilities.
Serving an industry	Equipment for newspapers	Perceiving needs	The marketing organization should include a highly skilled market research group to analyze and study the market and to identify potential areas for application of the company's product. A close relationship is required between marketing and production to permit effective responses to market assessment.
Operating a distribution system	Supermarket chain	Logistical efficiency	The supermarket chain is an efficient distribution system if it is intelligently aimed at a profitable segment of the market. The organization needs to be designed so that it can make quick responses to moves of competitors as well as the changing tastes of its customers. Pricing decisions are an important factor and responsibilities should be assigned on a regional basis to allow meeting competition. Some other merchandising decisions need to be made on a regional basis and some on a company-wide basis. The decision-making structure must recognize the various requirements that influence its viability.

Capitalizing on a possessed resource or production capacity	Ready-mix concrete plant	Establishing position in the market by geographic location and price structure	Profitability of individual accounts will vary depending upon the time of day customers wish to tie up our delivery equipment, the quantity they order, and the exact product. Competitors' prices vary from day to day and our interest in a particular block of business depends upon our current volume of orders. The operations manager needs to be in close contact with the sales department, the cost accounting department, and the dispatcher, so that he can maximize profitability and equipment utilization.
Serving a particular need	Building and operating apartments for the elderly	Specialization to develop in-depth understanding of needs	Attitudes concerning desired amenities change rapidly and planning which is done a year ahead of actual construction must stay in close touch with the market through market research. Also the profit on any one project is drastically affected by delays in completion of construction which increase the cost of interim financing and reduce the rent receipts. A close relationship is therefore required between construction and the leasing department.

including selling, market research, and operation of channels of distribution are interrelated and require close organizational ties.

The design concepts of the production function should also be evaluated by examining the basic production strategies. These are the commitments to a type of production process and to certain characteristics or qualities in that production process. Production process strategies may be generally classified as follows:

–Equipment especially designed and dedicated to a product, usually highly automated.

–Equipment specialized as to process but not as to product.

–General-purpose equipment utilized in combination with skilled workers.

–Application of a technology in which the equipment used is incidental.

–Production which is so simple and routine that it is not significant as a function.

The other basic strategy commitment to production characteristics is usually the means by which the production facility is made to relate to marketing strategy. Although the variety of these characteristics is broad, some of the more important ones are:

–Long runs of standardized products.

–Efficient handling of a variety of products with flexibility as to length of run.

–Responsiveness to customer requirements.

–Effectiveness in achieving specific results required by customers.

Illustrations of typical combinations of production strategies and design concepts are shown in Table B. For example, consider a metalworking company selling a variety of proprietary products. Its production facility consists of boring mills, semiautomatic turret lathes, gear cutters, and other powerful precision machine tools. Any given metal-cutting operation on a particular product can be efficiently and quickly performed. Considering the total variety of operations and products, however, the total task of accomplishing all operations to meet delivery dates and at the same time make efficient use of the machine tools is a complex operation. The production department needs a department or group which can perform the complex planning and record-keeping function needed to make efficient use of the

TABLE B
Typical production strategies and organization structure design concept

Basic production strategies			
Commitment to a production process that is:	*Operational characteristics*	*Example of type of company*	*Conceptual design that will effectively handle these key decisions or functions and provide the necessary coordination is required to:*
Automatic equipment designed for a specific product	Long runs of standardized products	Auto	Keep marketing separate from production. Give high-level status to demand forecasting. Centralize manufacturing decisions and create a detailed forward planning group. The production organization should be separated from planning and be highly structured to execute these plans.
Equipment specialized as to process	Efficient handling of specific operations on a variety of products	Metalworking process of a variety of products in med. vol.	Create a planning and control group responsible for planning and coordinating work through the shop on a day-to-day basis and design a close relationship between this group and planning. Place responsibility for reaching the best compromise between long runs and low inventories in between sales and production so that it can have an objective point of view.
General-purpose equipment and highly skilled production workers	Complete responsiveness to customer requirements on individual products	High-rise building construction	Keep the production organization flexible and unstructured to allow it to make decisions and solve whatever problems may arise in meeting customer requirements. Develop a close relationship between production and marketing to enable customer requirements to be transmitted in the most direct way possible.
Application of technology	Effectiveness in achieving special results desired by customer	Oilwell logging company	The production worker is in constant contact with customers performing the work under the technical supervision of engineering. Design the structure so that production, engineering, and marketing are properly coordinated at that point and so that decisions can be made in accordance with consideration of the overall situation at customers' site.

facilities. In addition, this group needs to be able to take an objective look at the pressures for long runs from manufacturing, as well as the need for keeping inventories low, and come up with the manufacturing quantities which represent the best compromise. All of these factors must be considered when the SITF evaluates the design concepts for the production function.

The SITF must also analyze the financial strategies which should be supported by organization structure. There are a wide variety of financial strategies which the SITF may find and examine. These relate to the type of financing, internal control, public relations, the type of investments to be sought, relations with the board of directors, and a host of other strategy concerns. A sample of these strategies and typical design concepts which might be associated with them is shown in Table C. For example, the President may be interested in establishing impeccable financial safeguards for his publicly held company. One strategy for accomplishing this might be to get the board of directors involved in financial matters in a meaningful way. Two concepts which will accomplish this are listed in Table C. In the first, a financial committee comprised of appointed members of the board of directors will be established to make certain financial decisions. Also, another committee composed of board members will be established to appoint and deal with the outside auditor. Both of these concepts have important implications for structural design.

There will be other strategies related to these functions and there will be other functions such as engineering that should receive the attention of the SITF. The priorities of these functions and the portion of the SITF's time spent on each of them will depend upon the SITF's perception of their relative importance.

Making the most of the human resources

Has the organization been designed to make the most effective use of the talents available?

Should specific responsibilities be increased or decreased to be in accord with the ability of the incumbent?

Is personal influence being used constructively and within the organizational structure?

Is the opportunity to exert influence without corresponding accountability being exercised with adequate responsibility?

TABLE C
Typical financial strategies and related design concepts

Financial strategy	*Typical design concepts*
1. Finance acquisitions through exchange of the company's stock.	Support stock price by providing high-level contact with brokerage community, screening data made public, and providing ready access to company for broker representatives. Allow president some time for personal dealings with brokers.
2. Finance growth through maximum use of long-term debt.	Provide high-level contact to maintain banking relations and develop a strong financial department to install and maintain effective financial controls.
3. Improve return on capital by relating managers' pay to the return on investment achieved in their divisions.	Set up financial specialists in each division to aid managers in analyzing the financial effects of their management decisions.
4. Maintain impeccable financial safeguards in a publicly held company by involving the board of directors.	Set up a board of directors' financial committee and define their responsibility for financial decisions. Set up an audit committee of members of the board of directors and define their relationship with the outside auditing firm.

Are groups of positions with close interactions designed holistically so as to take into account the combined talents of all of the executives involved?

A very old management myth which has not been completely dispelled holds that there is a theoretical structure which may be considered correct for each organization, without regard for the people who will carry out its responsibilities. The truth is that even after the most logical organizational structure has been developed, it usually must be modified in some manner. It may be designed to accommodate existing strengths or weaknesses or even to accommodate the interests and personal preference of the top executives. At the same time, one must be ready to acknowledge that the basic characteristics of an executive may be so different from those required by the structure that his separation is desirable. For example, an executive who prefers a completely unstructured approach to administration would be totally out of place in an organization in which internal efficiency is critical. The organizational structure places a manager in a position to exert influence, but the power with which he does so is modified by the power of his personality. Although it may be logical to place one manager under another, it may not be possible because the superior does not have the personal influence which is required. The best known example of this difficulty exists in the United States Department of Defense where it is public policy that a civilian will reign over the military. In recent years, however, in spite of their legal authority, several of the Secretaries and Under Secretaries of the Navy, Army, and Air Force have been patently without influence over the generals and admirals and, therefore, totally unable to control the nation's defense machinery.

A major factor which should be taken into account in modifying an organization structure is influence. Influence is perhaps the least understood factor at work in the behavior of an organization. Because it is not understood, it is seldom dealt with on a conscious level in organizational design. The SITF should recognize that influence can be a powerful force in an organization although it may be unseen and unacknowledged. The SITF will have to look closely to find spheres of influence because they operate as readily outside as inside channels established by the organization. Influence may operate in opposition to, or in support of, organizational goals and it may operate between any two points in an organization in spite of what the organizational chart may show.

> A new president took office in a firm manufacturing business forms. As soon as he did so, he replaced the manufacturing vice president with a younger man who he felt would be more aggressive in modernizing manufacturing methods and controls. The old vice president was "elevated" to the position of senior vice president and placed in charge of a minor function. As it turned out, the new manufacturing vice president found it extremely difficult to bring about meaningful changes in his organization. He met resistance at every turn; and both he and the president became extremely frustrated. After a year with little progress, the president finally realized that the former vice president of manufacturing was at the heart of the problem. He had run the manufacturing department with an iron hand for over 20 years. All of the manufacturing department heads were still so much in awe of him that they continued to conform to his opinions about how things should be run even though organizationally they had nothing to do with him. He made it a point to let them know what he thought of the new methods and programs and this conduct so influenced them that they would not give these innovations a fair trial. The president correctly concluded that he had to remove the older man from the organization completely in order to be rid of the negative impact of his influence.

The opportunity to influence behavior without accountability deserves special attention from the SITF. Staff positions such as product manager or project manager, as well as outside consultants given special assignments, interact with other executives largely through the exercise of personal influence rather than direct authority. The danger represented by individuals in these positions is derived from their lack of accountability. They are not responsible for results, yet they may exercise a substantial influence over the results achieved. Whether the impact of the staff executive is good or bad, his influence affects actions and decisions despite the fact that their effect is not tied back to him.

Staff personnel, whose principal duties consist of making recommendations to superiors, exercise a particular quality of influence over important decisions. By various means they color presentations supposed to be objective in a manner which may significantly affect the entire pattern of a company's decision-making. They may filter out, or include, certain information according to their own biases or according to the known biases of the decision makers. For these reasons, managers who fill staff positions should be chosen very carefully. The executive placed in an influential staff position must warrant complete trust. An executive with an exceptional amount of personal power will not likely confine his activity to the areas in which he is assigned on the organizational chart. Measures should be taken to contain influence in its proper sphere. This can be done either by establishing controls or by increasing the distance (organizationally or spatially) between the points involved. It often happens that the influence to be exerted is based upon technological knowledge or skill and that the person possessing this knowledge does not have the necessary personal power. Here his influence must be supported by his superior. It is well for the manager to examine all points at which influence is exerted officially and decide whether the interaction of influence between the individuals involved is reasonably well balanced. If it is not, he must take the necessary steps to achieve a proper balance.

Beyond this, there are a variety of ways in which the structure may be modified to suit the talents of existing personnel. An executive with unusual strength may have the ability to handle more functions than the current organization structure assigns to him. It is certainly in order, in such cases, to combine additional functions under him so that his talent can be fully utilized, unless, of course, this violates some important functional logic. It is also appropriate to *divide* functions and make positions smaller and more manageable for executives whose talent is limited.

If it is logical to design individual executive positions to suit individual characteristics, it is even more logical to design an entire set of positions to make the best use of the combined talents of a total management team. The SITF should examine the functions being performed as a group and evaluate their total design. Psychological characteristics which can be reliably measured include the intellectual capacity to deal with problems, the general manner of relating to other people in the organization at different levels, and the types of activity which interest and stimulate the executive. By carefully assessing the characteristics of an entire management group and comparing them with the characteristics required by the total job to be done, a number of organizational arrangements capable of strengthening the group as a team will be readily seen. For instance, the rules for determining where decision making should take place may indicate one thing, while an assessment of psychological characteristics may suggest another. It may be logical for one executive to make a certain decision when only his possession of facts and his responsibilities are taken into account. It may be logical for his superior to make the final decision, however, if the superior's intellectual characteristics are better suited. There are many instances of managers who are qualified to handle the day-to-day affairs of their jobs, but who do not have the ability or experience necessary for some of the larger decisions involved. Despite their limitations, they can still be productive if given appropriate support in the decision-making area.

In companies faced with a need for new managers, the SITF should determine if the organization structure has been designed to aid in producing these new managers.

CONCLUSION

In evaluating the organization structure the SITF will recognize that structure, itself, is no more than about half of that which should be considered in evaluating total organization. Structure is, after all, an influence on the behavior of individual managers. And unless those managers themselves are also measured against the concepts which are required for the success of the company, the job of evaluation of the organization is only half accomplished.

3

Concept audit of management

The concept audit has a very special task in relation to managers. The conceptual design of an organization structure or a system can be highly visible but the concepts by which a manager manages, being very personal, may not be easy to uncover. They are nevertheless important because how a manager manages within any given structure determines more definitely than anything else how effectively the corporation's human resources are used to execute its strategies. This is true because in his work of managing others the manager not only determines whose talent will be applied to a particular task, but just as importantly he is a primary factor in the level of enthusiasm and dedication which will be applied to the task. The vitality of an organization is affected in an important way by the style of its managers. The effectiveness with which the manager manages other managers is obviously dependent upon his own personal characteristics such as charisma and other intangibles; but it is also dependent to an important degree upon certain concepts of managing which the SITF should examine and evaluate.

This chapter deals with these concepts and how the SITF should go about evaluating their applicability to particular situations. The SITF will find there are two general categories into which these concepts fall. The first category is one dealing with manager quality. More specifically, it is suggested that the SITF approach "manager quality" in terms of how managers conceptually relate their subordinates to position requirements. Regardless of the technical assistance which managers may receive from the personnel department, they must assume the initiative and major responsibility for the deployment of the management talent under their control. A conscious development of the concepts by which this is done will enhance whatever intuitive ability of this nature the manager may possess. The SITF should not give the impression that it is evaluating individual managers since this would change the basic nature of the audit away from that of evaluating concepts.

In the second category to be dealt with in this chapter are concepts concerning how a manager relates to his subordinates. Again, the quality of these relationships is somewhat dependent upon such intangible characteristics as the manager's personal warmth or his personality in general, and they cover a full spectrum of interrelationships from purely social and subjective to purely business and objective. Superimposed upon this basis of personality, however, are certain procedures or approaches which the manager can employ to improve his effectiveness.

The concepts involved in these interrelationships constitute a major portion of the manager's style and they are susceptible to review by the SITF. The concepts of style discussed in this chapter are primarily related to decision making and communications.

Corporate strategy

What corporate strategies are dependent upon management style and management qualities?

What are the corporate attitudes that must be reflected in manager attitudes?

Are managers receptive to and interested in change?

Is there a special requirement for risk takers, specialized professionals, or other recognizable types of managers?

All strategy is executed by managers. Strategy may be brilliantly conceived; but until the necessary action by managers actually takes place, it is an abstract idea. More than mechanical action is usually required to execute strategy—it takes a certain spirit of aggressiveness or competitiveness. In fact, a major strategy of the corporation may be to sustain a corporate attitude of aggressiveness with some special orientation. Corporate attitude refers to the collective attitudes of a company's managers. If all or even most of a corporation's managers fervently desire innovation, cost reduction, improved methods, or any other achievement that requires a high rate of change, chances are that such change will occur. At least the SITF may be sure the converse will be true—no significant changes can take place in a company unless the managers desire their occurrence. The existence of these corporate attitudes is to a major extent a function of management style and of certain basic qualities inherent in the managers.

> IBM is known and held up to the world at large as an outstanding example of a successful corporation. Among its many notable characteristics one stands out with particular distinction—its "corporate attitude" of aggressive marketing. IBM has rigid specifications for the type of young men accepted into its marketing organization. They carefully screen, train, and manage these young men to fit the IBM mold. The result is an IBM attack force that is so persistent, so pleasant, so businesslike, so dedicated to the proposition that IBM is the only answer to any problem, so eager to surpass its quota, that it is one of the best marketing organizations the world has ever seen. Its corporate attitude is one of aggressive marketing.

Attitudes are intangible, of course. But the SITF must gain an understanding of what attitudes actually exist in order to evaluate fully the management style which brings them about. The SITF can gain considerable insight into what these attitudes are by interviewing a representative sample of managers. Various corporate attitudes may be desirable, depending upon the strategies to be executed, but one of the most common that the SITF will find of interest relates to the pace of change required in the company. In most corporations a high rate of change is synonymous with vitality. In such companies the SITF will need to know:

1. Are managers defensive about their actions and performance? Do managers feel compelled to think about how to cover themselves in case someone looks into their operations?
2. Are managers willing to take risks and make courageous decisions?
3. Are managers interested in and do they accept good ideas for improvements that come from outside their own departments?

4. Do managers initiate changes based on the advantages to be gained rather than on the necessity to react to competition or critical conditions?

The SITF can also assess the aggressiveness of the corporation directly by examining the rate of change introduced over a period of several years or by considering its typical method of competing. While there is no precise manner in which to describe an implicit attitude, the SITF will usually be able to get a pretty clear idea of what exists by observing what a company is actually doing.

The SITF may be dealing with certain strategies that can be implemented directly through care in choosing the kinds of managers or management candidates hired. Examples of management "types" which might correspond directly with strategy are: risk takers, professionals, or technicians. Choice among these "types" predicates desire for a particular result. Another example of a strategy that could be implemented directly with the kinds of managers hired would be to increase the pace at which a management group is being upgraded by switching the selection emphasis from a development program to a plan for hiring experienced managers from the outside.

Utilizing management resources

How well are manager capabilities matched with position requirements?

A major skill which a top manager must have is the ability to place his people in the right positions and to modify those positions so that man and position are a perfect fit. It has already been stated that he can be assisted in this function by the personnel department or by a psychologist. But the ultimate responsibility for understanding position and individual and putting them together effectively belongs to the manager.

To a major extent a manager's ability to do this will depend upon his intuitive grasp of the qualities of his subordinates. This ability, of course, will be beyond the scope of the SITF observation. A manager's intuitive perceptions can be improved upon, however, if he makes a practice of conceptualizing about manager qualities and how they relate to the work to be done. The SITF can determine fairly accurately to what extent this is being done by interviewing the individual managers. Once the operating concepts are known, the

SITF can evaluate their relevancy. Some of these concepts concerning manager qualities are relevant in almost any corporate circumstance.

Intellectual qualities

Is the need for conceptualizing skill recognized adequately at each management level?

The SITF may or may not find it productive to get into the question of matching manager intelligence with position complexity. The SITF should, however, look into the concept of relating a manager's conceptualizing ability to his position level. It has been noted that superior top-level managers usually have a special manner of thinking about operational functioning and problems. This manner can perhaps best be described as a highly developed style of *thinking conceptually.* There are several reasons why this is true. A concept comprises the manager's mental representation of the systems and subsystems with which he must deal; and conceptualizing is the thought process by which he transforms a myriad of seemingly unrelated facts into a system which can be understood and dealt with as a whole. This makes it possible for him to deal with an unlimited number of factors simultaneously by identifying unifying patterns and creating useful generalizations. Unless the manager has the ability to abstract these generalizations, it is necessary for him to deal with each individual factor or situation separately—a heavy burden on his time. Further, since a concept ties individual elements together into an integrated system which allows the conceptualizer to comprehend the operation of the system as a whole system, the operation or existence of individual elements may then be seen in relation to the whole. This overview reveals the relative importance or contribution of the individual elements in proper perspective. This is highly significant knowledge for the manager because it establishes priorities for action.

The central element of any business concept is the ultimate purpose of the system. Because the concept relates individual elements to the overall system, it shows their relation to its overall purpose. This connection indicates the true role of individual elements with greater clarity than would a statement dealing with procedure or technique. It should be clear from this discussion that conceptual thinking provides the manager with important insights into his organization as well as a certain balance in his perspective. The Association of Consulting Management Engineers has described this balance in perspective as follows:

> It is useful to view the institution as an operating system as a whole. One thing characterizes all genuine social systems like the business enterprise; namely *interdependence.* The whole of the system is not necessarily improved if one particular function or part is made more efficient. In fact, the system may well be damaged thereby or even destroyed. In some cases, the best way to strengthen the system may be to weaken a part—to make it less precise or less efficient or to inject imbalance or risk to make it significantly different from what it was. What matters in any system is the performance of the whole. This is the result of growth and dynamic balance, adjustment and integration rather than of more technical efficiency.

The SITF should explore the understanding by managers of the importance of conceptualizing. They should also determine the manner in which conceptualizing ability is being related to position level. The following table shows this relationship in a simplified form.

The concept of experience

Are experience specifications stated in terms of time or in terms of meaningful exposure?

Experience is typically specified in terms of elapsed calendar time. The SITF should recognize that a concept of experience which would be more useful to managers in assigning their personnel would be experience specified in terms of meaningful experiences. For example, the experience specification for a controller might include "two experiences of coordinating an annual manufacturing budget" and "complete responsibility for making cash projections and short-term cash investments." The experience specifications for a personnel manager might include the experience of "participating in the design of a job classification system" and "the development and training of a class on interviewing applicants." This approach emphasizes the quality rather than the quantity of experience, and although it requires a more detailed analysis the value of the information added would make it worth considering, especially on difficult and important positions. The concept is not only useful in making placement decisions but also in the design of on-the-job experience portions of manager development training.

Level	*Description of position*	*Level of conceptualizing abilities*
Lower-level managers	Concerned primarily with supervising operations with fixed procedures. Deal with factual data and make yes or no decisions based on fixed decision rules.	Understand procedures but not rationale upon which they are built. Can learn to follow an established set of rules for making decisions. Must obtain assistance for nonroutine problems.
Middle managers dealing with other managers and developing procedures and systems.	Solve problems in the general conceptual area in which they operate. Coordinate unstructured and complicated operations in achieving an organization's goals. Understand the functional relationship of each operation unit to the overall goal and control their operations to achieve this end. Apply techniques to difficult problems.	Understand concepts and typically think in terms of concepts; can solve complicated problems without fixed decision rules.
Top, policy-making managers.	Set goals for the organization. Foresee the possibilities of problems and make basic changes in the design or operation of the company to prevent the occurrence of problems.	Understand concepts that are currently in existence. Recognize the application of a concept found in an organization to the operation of another. Develop new concepts to fit new situations and strategies.

Manager attitudes

What basic manager attitudes are required for key positions?

The SITF should examine the concepts involved in specifying the manager qualities needed for individual jobs. Perhaps the most useful function the SITF can perform in this regard is to evaluate how well the concepts describe actual position requirements. One important family of manager qualities which may be particularly useful to the SITF are those dealing with a manager's basic attitudes toward himself and his environment. Regardless of the manager's level of intelligence or his other capabilities, these attitudes determine his basic approach to the work of managing and, in a large measure, his fitness for handling a particular job. These attitudes are basic because they are relatively fixed in his personality and are not usually changed by the typical development program or the normal relationship between himself and his supervisor. The SITF should prepare a list of basic attitudes that it feels are appropriate managerial qualities. In the list that follows, the attitudes are expressed by defining the two extremes of a spectrum. The extreme referred to as the high end is the basic attitude that would normally be considered the most effective one for the top manager of a corporation. The opposite of that attitude is expressed on the "low" side of the table. A corporate president or chief executive officer would not necessarily have all of the basic attitudes on the "high" side of the table, but the more of them he has the more likely he is to be suited for that position. The attitudes expressed on the "low" side are not necessarily bad; but it so happens that a president or a manager with broad general responsibilities would probably not be well suited to his position if very many of his basic attitudes were on that end of the spectrum. There are of course many positions for which the attitudes described on either end of the scale are entirely appropriate. The SITF can examine other specific positions and develop a list of basic attitudes that would fit them.

Management style

What management style will create the attitudes and produce the performance critical to this company?

Management style is the sum of the manager's relationships with his subordinates and the methods he uses to manage those subordinates.

Basic manager attitudes related to position requirements

High	*Low*
1. Deals with abstract concepts as well as concrete facts and circumstances.	1. Deals only with concrete facts.
2. Sees himself as a causative agent responsible for his own well being and success.	2. Sees himself as a responder–a victim of circumstances or subject to the will of higher authority.
3. Approaches problems realistically and rationally.	3. Approaches problems from the standpoint of his philosophical belief or his value system.
4. Understands the perspectives of others that are different from his own.	4. Cannot understand the perspectives of others.
5. Understands the infinite variety of qualities and characteristics in the people and circumstances with which he must deal.	5. Categorizes everything with which he must deal as either black or white–does not recognize shades of grey.
6. Understands and can deal with uncertainty.	6. Uncomfortable in conditions of uncertainty and has difficulty in making decisions about which he cannot predict the outcome with certainty.
7. Tolerates opinions that are at variance with his own and makes decisions objectively in the face of strong opposition.	7. Prefers consensus of opinion and likes to believe that his decisions satisfy everyone.
8. Is concerned with the end results to be achieved.	8. Overly concerned or preoccupied with appearances or with techniques.
9. Maintains a balanced perspective upon the interests of all parties involved–such as employers, stockholders, and the public.	9. Sees things only in terms of his own interests.

Aside from attitudinal relationships such as friendliness, respect, warmth, and the like, management style is comprised of three types of interrelationships which the SITF can analyze conceptually. The basic relationships which the SITF will wish to analyze are:

–The relationship between managers and their subordinates in decision making.

–The manager's most appropriate mode of communicating with subordinates concerning performance levels.

–Methods available to managers for learning about subordinates' attitudes and skills.

Before discussing these conceptual areas the general basis upon which they should be evaluated will be examined. Much popular writing by behavioral scientists has appeared during the past few years concerning such matters as job enrichment, participative management, self-actualization, and a host of management techniques designed to enrich the lives of workers at all levels. The writers on these subjects have been biased in assuming that workers are bored by their jobs and that this is primarily a social problem which must be solved by corporate managers. They are biased not because there may or may not be such a social problem, but because it is not placed in the proper perspective alongside the equally important problem of productivity. The level of productivity in the United States in general and in individual companies in particular is not so high that even the most "humanitarian" of managers can afford not to be vitally concerned about productivity. The quality of work in modern companies deserves improvement, but in both its humanization *and* its productivity.

In evaluating management styles built around humanist concerns, the SITF needs to have a very clear idea about how they relate to corporate goals. First of all, they should realize that humanist management methods are not necessarily compatible with increasing productivity. It is entirely possible that making a job more interesting may actually make it *less* productive.

> The president of a medium-sized life insurance company was heavily committed to participative management. His commitment was based on close personal relationships with the other officers and department heads, with whom he had a lifetime relationship. He valued these relationships more than he valued a high rate of progress for the company. That is, he would settle for an annual growth rate of 3 percent rather than fire the agency director and hire a new one who could achieve 10 percent. Where expense ratios were found to be higher than industry norms, he adhered to a group decision not to make cost-cutting moves because it would "destroy morale" within the company. On the other hand, the president knew where to draw the line and he made sound decisions where the company's safety or continued existence (as opposed to progress) were at stake. This president did not fool himself. He knew what his priorities and goals were, and he acted accordingly. His attitude is theoretically justified, of course, if one is concerned only about the current peace of mind of the

> executive group under the protective participative umbrella. A broader perspective, however, may indicate that the best interests of stockholders, policyholders, and even the employees are not being prudently looked after under such a philosophy. What would happen, for example, if unforeseen circumstances suddenly necessitated reserve strength that the company and its executives did not have?

The SITF should not be confused in related situations. It may be that the corporation does indeed have genuine humanist goals; but the SITF needs to understand the priorities of such goals as corporate democracy in comparison with others such as productivity.

Manager/subordinate interrelationships

How democratic can the organization be?

Have the decisions which can be group decisions been carefully identified?

The most pronounced sociological phenomenon of our age is the demand that the young and the inexperienced be allowed to participate in the decisions of the organization or institution of which they are a part. This demand is taking its toll in business organizations where many older managers are resisting pressures to make their operation more democratic, and the new graduates are looking away from that kind of leadership toward organizations willing to shed some of the traditional power held over their members. The issue tends to become more and more sharply drawn as a conflict between an autocratic and a democratic management style. If the SITF attempts to evaluate management style in terms of these opposing alternatives, it faces a very emotional issue and will not be considering the full range of management style concepts. First of all, the SITF should recognize that there is at least one other basic type of management style in decision making and that in a particular company a blend of concepts may be the most rational basis for setting style. That is, the SITF should be able to evaluate the decision-making process relative to the types of decisions to be made and the particular interests that are at stake. Before making such evaluations, however, the SITF should understand an important distinction between two types of "autocratic style."[1] A writer on parental styles

[1] D. Baumrind, "Authoritarian Vs. Authoritative Parental Control," *Adolescence*, vol. 3, 1968, p. 263.

of mothers has described the two styles, authoritarian and authoritative, in a manner which also applies to managers:

> The authoritarian parent as she is generally described in the literature attempts to shape, control, and evaluate the behavior and attitudes of the child in accordance with a set standard of conduct, usually an absolute standard, theologically motivated and formulated by a higher authority. She values obedience as a virtue and favors punitive, forceful measures to curb self-will at points where the child's actions or beliefs conflict with what she thinks is right conduct. . . . She does not encourage verbal give or take, believing that the child should accept her word for what is right.
>
> The authoritative parent as she appears in my studies also attempts to direct the child's activities but in a rational, issue-oriented manner. She encourages verbal give and take, and shares with the child the reasoning behind her policy. She values both expressive and instrumental attributes, both autonomous self-will and disciplined conformity. Therefore, she exerts firm control at points of parent-child divergence, but does not hem the child in with restrictions. The authoritative parent affirms the child's present qualities, but also sets standards for future conduct. She uses reason as well as power to achieve her objectives. She does not base her decisions on group consensus or the individual child's desire; but also, does not regard herself as infallible or divinely inspired.

In management the *authoritarian* type of manager is not only power-oriented but also imposes a value system on his subordinates which they may not accept, may even rebel against. It is not difficult to argue against the results of such a style. Authoritative style, on the other hand, places major emphasis on results and the development of subordinates. This is clearly a style that is oriented toward the welfare of the organization. This is also the style that is most properly contrasted with a participative management style which, in its extreme form, makes decisions on the basis of a purely democratic vote. In contrast to authoritative style its orientation is strictly toward the interest of the members. Unless an organization exists solely for the benefit of its members (which is obviously not the case in a business corporation), there is no assurance that the interests of the members are parallel with the interests of the organization. Nor is there any assurance that if their interests were parallel, the members at large would have the perspective necessary to make decisions in the best interest of the whole. The SITF will soon see that it would be illogical to allow decisions that are critical to the welfare of the organization to be decided on a completely democratic basis. At the other extreme there are, however, decisions which do not affect the organization in a critical manner but which members feel are critical to them. Here again, logic would indicate that such decisions should be democratic. In between these two extremes are decisions which impact both the company and its members as separable units, and the SITF will see that it is a matter of judgment as to the weight to be given the respective parties in these instances. In certain cases what is meant by participation may have to be changed. Members may be allowed to speak out on a matter while the manager will have final say after taking their opinions into account. A valid form of participation, not often recognized in decision-making, is one in which the opinions or interests of corporate managers are conscientiously weighed and considered but not followed unless they point to a decision in the interest of the corporation as a whole. By just being heard and having their opinions considered, the managers become a part of the decision-making process in a meaningful way even though they are not allowed to vote.

In summary, the SITF should examine decision-making concepts as they apply to different types of decisions. There are two other factors that should be evaluated in this connection. One is that a manager must have a certain level of self-confidence and self-assurance if he is to allow a decision to be made by his subordinate and in contradiction to his own preference. He must also be courageous and willing to make unpopular decisions when the welfare of the corporation is at stake.

Finally, the SITF should recognize that the decision-making process sets the scene for an even more important phase of the manager/subordinate relationship—the manager's communication with subordinates concerning their performance. In the process of listening to their views, regardless of how the decision is finally made, the manager learns how his subordinates think, feel, and react. This information is essential to the manager in developing an effective relationship with them. If, in addition, the manager can carry out the decision-making process in such a way as to cause his subordinates to feel they have contributed to the process, they are more likely to be in a receptive mood when he communicates with them about their performance.

Subordinates' performances

How should managers communicate with employees regarding performance?

What is the minimum satisfactory level of performance?

What should the manager do when performance standards are not met?

Perhaps the most critical element in the interrelationship between a manager and his subordinate is the manner and substance of his communications with them concerning their performance. Here again the SITF must be careful not to become confused by popular management writing. From such authorities they could easily gain the impression that a manager should not demand or require anything from his subordinates. They might get the idea that a good manager does not have to communicate the level of performance he desires because if he is good he can *inspire* a higher level than required. There is a certain truth in this idea. The problem, however, is that inspiration is almost always offered as an alternative to requiring performance. This is illogical. The completely effective manager will incorporate some of both in his management style. He will adopt methods which he hopes will inspire high performance, but at the same time he will establish a floor *under* performance below which he will be intolerant.

Some managers cannot be inspired to perform at high levels. Not all managers are capable of or interested in self-fulfillment. And, quite obviously, not all managers are capable of performing at high levels. As a practical matter, managers need a method of taking a stance with their subordinates on the subject of "minimum level of satisfactory performance." In evaluating operative concepts involving management style, the SITF should determine whether communications concerning level of performance deal with both a "high" level and "minimum satisfactory" level. Not dealing satisfactorily with the latter inevitably leads to various degrees of weakness within an organization. The other key point in general evaluation of management style is the clarity with which the manager communicates his posture on performance levels. The only way the SITF can evaluate this communication is by interviewing both the manager and his subordinate and seeing how well their viewpoints agree on what has been communicated. The SITF should obviously also evaluate the concepts around which the performance communicating methods themselves have been designed. There are a number of these methods which may have been adopted by the company or which the SITF will wish to evaluate because they think they ought to be considered by the company. Some of these which deal with the minimum or required side of performance are performance standards and firing practices.

There is a general misunderstanding of the appropriate use of performance standards. They are often criticized as being inhibitors of high levels of performance. Prevalent attitudes as frequently expressed in business journals can be summarized as follows:

> Performance standards traditionally established by management or its engineers are an attempt to dictate a high level of performance by employees (at all levels). Since the employees do not participate in setting these standards, they are resentful of them and serious conflicts develop. The employees attempt to "beat" the system by holding back and producing barely enough to get by. This condition results in productivity levels substantially lower than employee capacity. Employees would be motivated to higher levels of performance if management would stay out of the standards setting business and allow them to establish their own goals.

The error lies in the assumption that performance standards represent a high level of performance, whereas their true function is to state the minimum level of performance that will be acceptable.

Upon understanding the real purpose of performance standards the SITF can concentrate on evaluating the basis for establishing "minimum satisfactory levels." Two basic concepts are generally used in this exercise. One is the minimum level necessary for the corporation to meet its goals. This basis is most applicable to key executives whose levels of performance can be stated in terms of corporate sales goals, profit, rate of growth, etc. The other concept is more generally applicable to all employees including production and clerical: the level that the normally qualified employee can meet working at a normal pace. For production and administrative workers this definition has achieved a universal meaning among industrial engineers and can be applied fairly uniformly from company to company. For other types of personnel it often can be established only through the exercise of judgment. SITF should in no way consider, however, that this makes it a less valid way of setting standards or less essential for higher levels of managers.

The SITF should also determine corporate reactions when performance standards are not met. A manager's commitment to performance means that he must be willing to fire a subordinate. Firing is a taboo subject, but it is a bona fide method for motivation and should not be denied to the manager. It is seldom discussed, and in reading management literature one might think firing never occurred. It is as though firing were just too terrible to think about. Firing of course, is something every manager must know how to do properly. Some modern managers object to it because they are "sensitive" to the feelings of their subordinates and would rather endure substandard performance than hurt one of them.

> Even Robert E. Lee was guilty of failing to replace a bad performer. General Lee would very likely have won the battle of Gettysburg if General Longstreet had attacked General Meade as Lee ordered him to do. General Longstreet, not knowing the strategic importance of the point he was to attack, decided on his own initiative that his losses would be too great and did not make the attack that Lee was relying on. Instead of replacing Longstreet, Lee, Southern gentleman that he was, accepted the blame himself, saying that his orders to Longstreet should have been clearer and more emphatic. As kind and gallant as Lee's actions were, the magnitude of his error was increased by the dramatic circumstances of war. In a similar situation which occurred very soon after Gettysburg, General Longstreet repeated the same error and the South paid for it with the loss of many lives and eventually the war.

The manager who requires performance may very well be sensitive to the feelings of subordinates, but he also realizes that the corporation and all those dependent upon it are jeopardized by poor performers. Experience shows that a manager who is not performing satisfactorily will usually benefit in the long run by being removed from a position he cannot handle. If the man is poorly motivated, his removal from the job may be what is required to make him realize how necessary it is for him to perform according to his talents. It is important to the well being of the inept manager that he be replaced as early in his career as possible, while he still has an opportunity to find his niche.

Another reason managers sometimes do not believe in firing is that they have a misconception about their function as managers. They sincerely believe that management is "managing people" or that management is "getting things done through other people." The statement is made of course to emphasize the importance of personal relationships, but the manager who too literally believes and acts according to this philosophy cannot *require* performance. It is after all the operating results which count, and not how diligently one tries to remake managers who are not qualified to handle their jobs. Effective management is a means to an end and not the end itself.

Many managers have found themselves in the unhappy situation of having to replace a 50- or 60-year-old manager who should have been moved into a different kind of position years before. In most cases, after a brief period of hurt pride, a man removed from a job he cannot handle finds himself much more satisfied in a job that is matched with his capabilities.

Management by objectives (MBO)

Is there an effective means for allowing managers to establish their own specific goals?

Is the goal-setting procedure such that managers become truly committed to the achievement of their goals?

Are individual manager goals aptly tied in with corporate goals?

A management-by-objectives program can be one of the most effective means of focusing a manager's attention on the high side of performance.

Often MBO programs are regarded only as a means of management development. To use the MBO program solely for management development is to fail to utilize completely an effective management tool. Another basis upon which the SITF may evaluate operating MBO concepts is whether there is visible concentration on meaningful goals as opposed to measurable goals. Some MBO proponents have stressed the need for quantitative measurement of goals. This procedure has led to the establishment of goals because they can be measured and not because their achievement is necessarily needed. Quantitative goals are easier to deal with, but the SITF will be most concerned about evaluating goal quality itself.

Performance reviews

Are performance reviews fully utilized for developmental and motivational purposes?

Performance reviews are one of the most important instruments in aiding the manager to obtain high-level performance. Nevertheless, the SITF may find that performance reviews are not handled according to an overall, well-thought-out concept or even that they are not performed at all. The primary concepts that should be considered are:

1. Does the review procedure provide feedback to the subordinate that will serve both his development and as corrective action on the conduct of the company's affairs?
2. Does it bring about a conscious evaluation process in the manager of both his individual subordinates and the state of development in his organization as a whole?
3. Does it aid in the process by which the manager learns more about the basic attitudes and capabilities of his subordinates in order that he may use such information both in managing those persons and in fitting them into his organization?

The evidence that the performance evaluation practice is or is not used for these purposes should be available to the SITF from the notes and records that document the performance review sessions.

CONCLUSION

The "management" of an organization consists of the personnel who carry out its duties and the methods and style they employ in doing so. Their total effectiveness will depend on how well the individual managers are matched with their positions and on how much of their collective abilities they apply effectively to their work. The matching and predetermined application of these talents in a purposeful manner is the aim of the design concepts of management. If, in addition to management concepts, the management compensation concepts are well conceived, the management body can be extremely effective.

4

Management compensation

The audit of organization structure and managers within an organization often reveals that *human resources* are among the company's most valuable assets. Corporate managers determine strategies and monitor their execution. They are, therefore, essential to the achievement of corporate goals. Yet, despite the obvious criticality of human resources, their monetary "value" is so appallingly difficult to measure that executive compensation stands apart as one of the least productive utilizations of corporate financial resources. Whether or not a company is able to utilize compensation effectively as a significant contribution to the execution of strategy is often dependent upon underlying management attitudes toward compensation. Typically, the attitude of management falls into one of three broad categories:

> The first attitude: *Compensation has a management purpose*
>
> Compensation has a definite purpose which is to serve as another means of supporting the achievement of overall corporate objectives. We do not attempt to set our compensation levels at the highest, lowest, or even at the average market levels as a matter of principle. Rather, we think in terms of setting them at the "right" level for what we are trying to do.

This causes us to pay quite a bit of attention to what is going on in the field of compensation in general and to think through carefully what we expect to accomplish with our plan.

The second attitude: *Compensation as a nuisance*

Compensation is essentially a controllable expense which we must keep at the lowest possible level. We do this by withholding increases until the costs of turnover begin to be excessive. We usually react quickly when other companies attempt to steal our employees by increasing their salaries and by discussing the many fine opportunities available to them if they stay with our company. Control of salary costs begins with recruiting. We normally hire employees who do not have employment. They do not demand top salaries and thus we start out with salary costs that are below the market.

The third attitude: *Compensation as ego satisfying*

Compensation is our means of sharing with our employees. Our business is prosperous and we do not need nor do we wish to be stingy in paying salaries. On the contrary, our philosophy is to be generous in sharing our profits with our employees and, most especially, we intend to be generous to those who have been loyal employees for many years. Our salary scale is somewhat higher than the market and consequently our employees are very loyal and seldom leave us.

The third attitude may (but does not necessarily) derive from a genuinely humane attitude toward employees, and certainly this is not to be criticized. However, managers should not confuse this attitude with the attitude that compensation has a useful (as opposed to a benevolent) purpose to serve.

At the other end of the attitude range is the viewpoint that compensation is a necessary evil—a nuisance. Where this attitude exists, positive benefits from compensation are obviously neither sought nor achieved. This is, in fact, reflective of a very negative feeling concerning employees.

The first attitude is, of course, the most constructive and the most likely to lead to the design of an effective compensation plan. The key questions for the SITF to examine are: What strategies should the compensation plan support? What should be the general salary levels? What elements should be included in the total compensation plan and how shall the plan be applied to individual positions and managers? The answers will differ for each organization and must be based on fundamental concepts concerning compensation.

The compensation plan

What are the overall goals of the compensation plan?
What corporate strategies should the compensation plan support?
What values are established by the compensation plan?

The primary goal of the compensation plan is to support the achievement of overall corporate objectives. The SITF should, therefore, determine specific corporate goals as well as related strategies for achieving the goals and then see if they are supported by the compensation plan. If management talent, for example, represents a factor critical to corporate expansion or profitability, then typical strategies for satisfying the critical factor involve competing for management talent and motivating individual managers to achieve necessary levels of performance. These two strategies, in turn, *must* be supported by the compensation plan. It follows that the goals of the compensation plan will be to attract talented managers from outside the organization and to aid in developing managers within the organization. The compensation plan invariably has an important influence on the overall quality and progress of the management cadre as a whole. For example, a general movement upward within this group is usually desirable. New managers enter the company, develop, move up or move out, and are replaced. The rate of movement must not be so slow as to discourage ambitious managers and not so fast as to create chaos. New managers must be developed and made ready for promotion in a sequence which roughly corresponds to the rate at which they are needed by the company. The strategy for accomplishing this is to weed out inadequate managers, retire older managers, identify and promote good managers, and encourage all managers to take an interest in their own development.

In conducting the concept audit of a company's compensation plan, the SITF should attempt to determine the nature of the value system established by that plan. If pay scales are to be competitive, equitable, provide incentive for better than satisfactory performance, and recognize outstanding performance, the compensation plan must recognize and support "value contributing factors" associated with individual abilities and performances. While conducting the concept audit of compensation, the SITF must keep in mind that the value system is actually a subsystem of the compensation system, and must be just as sound conceptually.

The value system

What values are established by the compensation system?
What value contributing factors does the compensation plan recognize?

The compensation plan is much more than a means of establishing rates of pay for managers. It establishes a value system expressing not only the worth of a position but also the worth of its incumbent to the corporation. An underpaid manager is of more concern than the number of dollars involved because the manager's personal worth is at issue. A manager's progress, as well as his status within the corporation, is clearly (but not necessarily accurately) stated by his salary level. Unfortunately, salary structures often do a poor job of expressing value. Formal systems of job evaluation are typically thought of as measuring "the value of the job and not of the man." The "value of the job" may carry greater weight than the "value of the man" in lower-level and routine positions, but this is certainly not true in the higher and more complex jobs. Perhaps, in contradiction to "classical" management theory, positions are shaped to some extent by the managers who hold them, so that what the positions are worth to the corporation varies with individual capability to a greater degree than is allowed by typical salary schemes.

The SITF should determine whether the compensation plan has an adequate means of recognizing the *full range* of values associated with particular individuals:

> A company marketing several specialty items hired a new marketing director. They felt fortunate in having been able to hire him at only a slight increase in salary over that paid to the former marketing director. His ability to handle the job was soon proven. He motivated the sales force in such a manner that sales increased measurably. He ushered in new innovative approaches to the marketing function which produced tangible results. He launched an advertising campaign for a new product which resulted in that product's becoming the most profitable in the company's line. When both his superiors and his subordinates were questioned about his performance, they said, "His would be a hard act to follow. I don't know how anyone could fill his shoes."

The value of the position of marketing director when filled by this man could hardly be measured as it was when his predecessor held the position. The position took on new dimensions when a superior manager moved into the slot. This situation frequently develops. The compensation plan must be flexible enough to recognize that position values are seldom fixed. The value of a position may increase, or functions related to a position may decrease, in which case the position value may also decrease. It is, therefore, the job of the SITF to determine whether or not the compensation plan has an adequate means of recognizing the full range of values associated with not only positions, but also with the individuals who hold the positions.

Formal systems of salary evaluation are often faulty because of the factors they include or omit from their "evaluation system." The SITF will normally find two general factors that should contribute to the establishment of value. These factors are derived either from personal qualities which the manager must have to perform the job or from the job's potential impact on corporate objectives. If the SITF finds factors in use that cannot be related to either of these bases, it must be on guard to make sure the evaluation system is not based on an arbitrary set of values.

Values derived from "personal qualities" such as skill, knowledge, and experience are established mainly by competitive circumstances. These are the qualities or features "bought" with the system. Such qualities figure strongly in establishing the value of jobs that are especially vulnerable to executive raiders. Such qualities are usually treated in a fairly satisfactory manner in formal evaluation systems.

The second set of factors, involving a position's importance to corporate goals is sometimes handled well on an intuitive basis by individual managers; it is seldom handled adequately in formal evaluation systems. Matching position contribution with position salary level requires careful thought and the exercise of a high level of judgment. The evaluation is susceptible to logic, however, and is simplified by the fact that its primary aim is to establish internal equity among jobs. Because of this, position evaluation can be carried out by comparing the *relative* impact of different positions on goals rather than their absolute contributions. If a formal position evaluation system is in use, the SITF will find it much easier to examine the concepts involved than it will if individual salary levels are established intuitively. A word of caution concerning the design of such systems is in order. First, in dealing with job impact, the SITF should bear in mind that *susceptibility* of results to the manager's quality of management should be taken into account. A job may be very difficult, or it may involve the handling of large sums of money, for example, and yet not have a large impact on corporate goals because the results are not particularly affected by the quality of the management. Job impact, or the worth of a job, derives directly from the amount of control over results inherent in the job, and is measured by the results the manager is expected to accomplish.

Finally, the SITF should be careful in evaluating the concepts behind a formal position evaluation system so as to not overestimate the system's accuracy in establishing position value simply because it gives the appearance of offering great precision. Such systems tend to create the illusion that they express true and universal value. They merely establish relative value or internal equity, not absolute dollar value. Further, the SITF should understand that a firm's value scheme (even on a relative basis) is not created by its position evaluation system. The values are, or should be, already in existence in the company at the time the system is put into effect. The aim of the system is to capture these values and to make it possible for them to be applied consistently, from job to job. An important test of the validity of a new salary evaluation system is to compare the rankings produced by the system with the intuitive rankings by various managers within the company. If there is a wide divergence between these two, the system should be carefully reexamined. An informed executive's intuitive relative ranking of position value is usually fairly reliable.

Components of the compensation package

How should the SITF approach the "parts" of a compensation package in order to evaluate the whole?

The compensation system is, of course, composed of base salaries, bonuses or other incentive plans, and fringe benefits. The SITF must examine each component to evaluate the total compensation system. While major emphasis should, of course, be placed on salary levels, certain components of the compensation plan must be included in the evaluation, not for their positive contribution, but because of the negative impact which would be created by their omission.

Fringe benefits

How generous should the fringe benefit package be?

What problems will be caused by omission of a pension plan?

Fringe benefits such as pension plans, hospitalization, time off, and some forms of deferred compensation are considered in the management market to be essential to the compensation plan because they are *expected.* Many companies publicize their fringe benefit package when recruiting new managers as though they expect the package itself to attract management candidates. If the incidental nature of fringe benefits were better understood, a great deal of fringe benefit expense would be avoided. This is not to say that a company wishing to provide its employees with a superior fringe benefit program should not do so. It is merely an observation that fringe benefit programs superior to those of competitors are hardly noticed and buy very little advantage for any company in the marketplace for high-talent employees. On the other hand, the fringe benefit package should be no less than that of the competition because deficiencies are noticeable and cause negative responses. A proper objective for fringe benefit programs is that they have no impact either way, negative or positive! Fringe benefits should be made as inconspicuous as possible by making them similar to competing plans.

However, one component of fringe benefit packages deserves special mention. This is the pension plan. There are still many small and medium-sized companies which, for one reason or another, do not provide retirement income for their employees. At some time in the future these companies are going to face an unpleasant situation. Sooner or later a time comes when it is better for older executives to retire and move out. When a chief executive realizes that one of his managers has reached this point, he is faced with an agonizing decision: he must either dismiss him, with no means of support, or let him stay around and hope that he won't be too much in the way. A pension plan or other forms of retirement income are important because they allow for the renewal of the corporation's management group.

But extra fringe benefits are costly to a company if they have no real executive buying power. The SITF should determine whether any portion of the fringe benefit package represents such extra "frills." One benefit that does not necessarily belong in the frill category is stock options.

Stock options

Are stock options needed to attract and/or keep managers?

Management sometimes regards stock options as a "motivating response to performance" because, presumably, the value of the options goes up proportionately as the performance of the executive improves the lot of the company. In certain cases this may be a valid assumption; however, a more realistic view regards stock options as primarily a means of competing for managers. Stock options are sometimes the icing on the cake that attracts a manager, while other fringe benefits are taken for granted. But even for very top managers the connection between performance and stock price is difficult to establish. Further, prudent management must sometimes take a long-run view at the expense of present earnings. This confronts the executive having stock options with a conflict of interests. In evaluating the use of stock options, the SITF should make sure it understands why they are being used. It also should ascertain whether or not their cost has been properly analyzed.

Salary levels

What kind of managers does the company wish to attract?

How high should the salary level be to attract such managers?

At what level can the company afford to place its salaries?

What effect, if any, should a bonus or incentive plan have on base salaries?

Determining equitable, competitive, and meaningful salaries is one of management's most difficult tasks. The SITF can provide valuable insight because it, collectively, can observe salary levels with some objectivity. While salary levels must reflect an individual's responsibilities and "value" to the company, compensation concepts are often forgotten in the day-to-day tasks of administering a salary system. This often results from a failure to periodically monitor, upgrade, and evaluate the total configuration of salary levels within the management group. In evaluating concepts concerning salary levels the SITF must fully understand the type of manager needed by the company and, thus, the type of manager the compensation plan should attract.

A compensation plan will be one thing if it is designed to attract the entrepreneurial risk takers required in a land development company, and quite another thing if it is designed to attract managers oriented toward financial security. A plan aimed at attracting experienced and proven managers will be different from one aimed at recently graduated MBAs. A plan intended to attract creative, innovative, high-performance managers will include different features than one designed to attract good but not exceptional managers.

The SITF will find that, unless the company has well-developed concepts about the types of managers most appropriate for its tasks, the strategic design of the compensation plan will not effectively attract the type needed at prices the company can afford.

The argument for pushing salaries up toward whatever levels can be *afforded* is most relevant in the case of high-level executives. For lower executives with less profit impact, salary levels may be allowed to recede to something nearer to the competitive level. Even here, however, there is a danger in attempting to economize by holding down individual salary levels. Less talented managers are unable to assume heavy responsibility. Also, the ability to organize and manage other managers efficiently is one distinctive mark of a high-talent manager. The mediocre manager tends to operate on the principle of "one problem–one manager." For every new problem situation which arises, he creates a new position and assigns a separate manager to that position. Under these managers there is a proliferation of staff positions such as "Assistant to" and "Coordinator of," and thus a considerable increase in total salaries.

A typical criterion used in setting salary levels is that they should be as high as, but no higher than, the level necessary to attract the kind of managers needed. At first this seems to be a practical approach since it aims at minimizing costs. But by reason of one very important yet generally unrecognized factor, this is seldom the most effective basis for setting salary levels. Managers sometimes fail to recognize an important relationship between talent and the salary level required to buy talent. These two quantities do not increase at the same rate. Talent in the manager marketplace, or more accurately the result talent produces, increases at a faster rate than the salaries required to buy that talent. Examination of salary levels paid to chief executives within an industry will show, for example, that salary increases by about 20 percent as company size doubles. Theoretically, a company could hire a president capable of managing a company twice its size by merely increasing his salary 20 percent. If there is any doubt about the leverage of salary dollars, the following comparison should be convincing. A company could increase the base salary of its president from $60,000 to $72,000 and make a definite step upward in managerial quality. Assume that this company does a

$50,000,000 volume annually and has historically achieved a 7 percent net profit before taxes. A reasonable expectation for the improvement a superior manager could bring about is two percentage points in net profit plus other advantages, such as an increase in volume. The 2 percent improvement in net alone, however, is equal to $100,000 or eight times the salary increment. Although the example is somewhat simplistic, it indicates that the essential nature of the relationship between talent and results is such that the salary level which can be afforded may be much higher than is generally realized. Within reasonable bounds, the SITF will usually find that the most effective strategy for setting salary levels is: *Salaries should be set high enough to assure that high-performance managers are available; if there is any doubt as to whether salaries are high enough, they should be set still higher because it is poor economics to be on the low side.* This philosophy is also applicable to other decision-making executives whose performance can have a large impact on the company's performance. In fact, it would be possible to justify *any* reasonable salary level for a marketing or production executive based upon the benefit gained in going from the mediocre to the superior. The cost of a $50,000 executive, for example, is $20,000 per year more than that of a $30,000 executive, but this difference is almost insignificant when compared to the differences in profit that would typically be generated by the two executives.

Incentive programs and bonuses

Do incentive programs justify lower base salaries?

The question of the general level of salaries is complicated to some degree by the existence of bonus or incentive systems. Some companies deliberately establish their salary levels lower than those of their competitors and adopt a bonus arrangement to bring total compensation up. These companies are seldom successful in competing for high-talent managers. On the other hand, a frequently stated principle holds that base salary levels should be competitive even when there is opportunity for additional incentive compensation, and that such additional compensation should in no way be used to make up a deficit in a substandard base salary level. Actual practice in American industry, however, tends to contradict this principle. Surveys usually show that, within the same industry, base salary levels of successful bonus-paying companies are lower by about 10 to 15 percent than the salary levels of their non-bonus-paying competitors, but that their *total* compensation is 10 to 15 percent higher than that of non-bonus-paying companies. Most likely, there would be general agreement among the successful bonus-paying companies that base salaries may be permitted to be slightly lower than their competitors', provided there is sufficient bonus opportunity to allow total earnings to be substantially higher than their competitors'. The base salary level cannot be allowed to get too far out of line, however, because the base salary level, rather than total compensation, tends to be the perceived measure of value.

> This point was dramatically illustrated in a new multi-store retail company which had gone through its formative stages and was beginning to reach a more mature condition. Morale among managers was low, and newly trained managers were leaving to join the company's competitors. Corporate management was at a loss to understand this because total earnings of individual managers were very competitive and the earnings of many were as much as 20 to 25 percent higher than standard earnings in the industry. Although the company was quite young, it had hit upon a very effective formula for doing business and had enjoyed a rapid rate of growth in both profit and volume. Because of the risk involved to managers who joined the untried company initially, the original compensation plan was to pay very low base salaries plus a bonus of an unusually high percentage of profits, if any. The plan was highly effective in motivating profit performance because the personnel understood and were sympathetic with the new company's need for a low downside risk. As the company grew, however, managers became more aware of the base salary differential as compared to other companies and began to feel a lack of status or worth. They were actually embarrassed about their low base salaries in spite of their combined greater total earnings. The executives were satisfied when the compensation plan was changed to increase their base salaries, decrease their bonuses, and bring about a net reduction in their total compensation. In spite of the decrease, they now felt that the base salary was more equitable and reflected their true value to the company. Their sense of personal worth had been restored.

Compensation as a response to performance

Is compensation properly used as a response to performance?

One of the major concepts about compensation is that it is a means of establishing a system of job values, or a salary system which indicates the worth and status of positions. A complementary concept is that it is a means of creating personal motivation in individual executives through a perceptible financial response to results. Typically, this is achieved through a system of bonuses and salary increases. A hard-fought argument persists concerning the extent to which the intrinsic value of money motivates the effort of executives; some argue that other factors, such as greater participation in decision-making, the opportunity for self-actualization, increased status, or recognition, have the most lasting effect upon motivation. For purposes of understanding and designing a salary administration system the SITF should consider this argument as having only academic interest, because financial rewards *do* motivate executive achievement whether it be because of the intrinsic value of money or by reason of other factors attendent upon financial rewards. The detractors of financial motivation will find it difficult to convince the executive who has had the responsibility of administering executive salaries and who has had to solve problems caused when the amount or the timing of an increase misses the mark.

Executives generally agree that financial response is most effective in motivating performance when there is a clearly perceived relationship between the performance and the reward. The SITF will be interested in evaluating this relationship based on the time lag between performance and response as well as the equity between the magnitude of the response and the excellence of the performance. Effective response to performance requires the most objective and rational appraisal of performance that is possible. All of this is so obvious as to seem unnecessary of restatement, and yet many administrators seem not to take seriously the tying-in of performance with the frequency and size of salary increases. A few statistics gathered from a company's payroll history will give the SITF a very good indication of whether or not this has been the case. In each review period, patterns in granting increases may consistently indicate that a "proper" increase is 3 percent, 5 percent, or some other number. Actual performance levels are going to vary considerably among executives, however, and salary increases ought to display the same sort of variable distribution. Managers within a compensation system are quick to recognize when tenure and not performance is the basis for increases or bonuses, and can enlighten the SITF in this regard. Proportionate and timely response to performance is, therefore, an important influence which either inhibits or enhances performance.

The manager who wishes to correlate increases and bonuses with individual achievement is, however, faced with certain risks. No matter how skillful his attempts, his efforts may be interpreted as favoritism. It is best that he act with courage and recognize that, in the long run, it will be his actions rather than his pronouncements which reveal his policy concerning the connection between performance and reward. Some managers may not have a choice between increases or bonuses as a means of responding to performance because of policy decisions at a higher level or because their company's circumstances may prohibit the use of incentive compensation. For those who do have a choice, however, the question of what kind of response should be made to performance should be based upon an understanding of the fundamental differences between the two concepts. Bonus or incentive plans have the greatest value in motivating performance when it is the result, itself, which is to be emphasized. Salary increases, on the other hand, are the more effective response when it is the quality of management which is to be rewarded.

Bonuses as responses to performance

Should response to performance be related to results or to the manager's performance and development?

Bonuses that have the quality of being variable or impermanent, and of being associated with the immediate past, may or may not be effective in motivating performance, depending both upon the way they are administered and upon the characteristics of the managers involved. To fully understand the nature of bonuses, a distinction must be made between two different types of bonuses. The *first* type is the bonus directly related to the profit results of the company; this is a form of profit sharing.

Tying the bonus to "ability to pay" is an advantage for the company whose earnings are volatile and heavily dependent upon the manager's day-to-day performance. Such plans present the classical financial incentive situation in which the manager's rewards are directly related to results, good or bad. Since the amount of bonus is determined by the amount of profit and is not a personal recognition of a manager's performance by his superior it is very impersonal. Such bonuses tend to be regarded as a sharing in a specific result rather than an acknowledgment of the manager's personal contribution. In a sense, this form of bonus is the purest form of financial incentive since it requires the exercise of no judgment in its administration. It is on this point that behavioral scientists are apt to make the best case against its effectiveness as a motivator. No doubt only certain types of managers are interested and willing to risk a large part of their compensation on the results they are personally responsible for producing. Some feel it is too much of a gamble and others, unfortunately, look no farther than the next paycheck. For this type of bonus system to be effective, the managers must be entrepreneurial in spirit and they must be able directly and significantly to affect the profit results of the company. The latter requirement alone severely limits the number of executives within a given company for whom a profit-related bonus is appropriate. If it is extended to middle management, whose impact on profit is normally too indirect and seldom visible, the bonus system does not offer strong motivation and tends to be accepted by those managers as an impersonal *share* in profits to which, over some time, they come to believe they are entitled. Therefore, profit-sharing bonuses should be restricted to companies for which profitability is highly dependent upon day-to-day operations (as opposed to being dependent upon policy making and long range decision making) and within those companies to those executives who have direct and visible impact on profit. Such executives must be willing to take risks and depend upon their own personal performance for a large part of their compensation.

Bonus plans which are not tied in with profit performance by formula may be used by companies whose profits are sufficiently stable to assure the availability of funds. Such plans may be applied to all levels of executives. The key to making them successful is development of a meaningful relationship between performance and the bonus amount. This requires a careful definition of what constitutes meritorious performance and of the method by which it will be judged. It also requires a method of establishing the amount of bonus for a given level of performance. Experience indicates that a bonus on the order of 20 to 30 percent of base salary may be necessary to act as an effective stimulus for greater effort, although in some highly volatile industries bonus payments are traditionally 50 to 60 percent of total compensation. If the bonus is set at a high enough level to provide stimulus, and if performance is well defined, the bonus plan will affect performance to a significant degree. If the performance level that is required to earn the bonus cannot be clearly defined, the company may be better off without a bonus plan. The SITF should recognize that a key element in all bonus plans is that they be seen as pay or reward for very specific accomplishments. That is, they are paid in return for something and do not necessarily indicate general advancement for the recipient. They are most appropriate when the company wishes to achieve specific accomplishments or accomplishment levels, as opposed to emphasizing and encouraging executives development. Bonus systems are oriented toward *things.* They emphasize getting things done and are not particularly useful in developing management personnel. Bonuses may, in the short run, motivate a manager to developmental activity. In the long run, however, they are not the kind of response to performance which will motivate the manager's best developmental effort because they are pay for what he has done rather than for what he has become.

Salary increases as responses to performance

How should salary increases be matched with performance?

Salary increases have a quality of permanence because they are a promise of continued future payment. They therefore indicate a long-range appreciation of the executive's qualities as a manager. The executive tends to associate increases in salary with his increasing status and his personal rate of progress rather than, as in the case of bonuses, with specific acts or results. The basic concept, therefore, that should govern the granting of increases is that they are a primary means of motivating the manager's development. The visible evidence which brought the increase about may have been results, but the implication behind the granting of a salary increase is that it is warranted by the quality of management that brought about those results. Bonuses, on the other hand, are almost by definition a product of fate and, therefore, more dependent upon fortuitous circumstances than upon the executive himself and far less personal than the salary increase. The executive's tolerance for error in judgment regarding a bonus is greater than it is for salary increases because the bonus is less personally determined, and it is for a period which is past and gone. The salary increase, on the other hand, is more strongly associated with justice because it is related to evaluation of his worth and he must continue to live with it in the future. In order to be fully motivated for future development, therefore, the executive requires that his performance be uniquely and justly recognized. This obviously requires a very effective and flexible means of matching salary increases with performance. Management's difficulty in doing this stems from two sources. First, managers lack confidence in their ability to judge differences in performance with the accuracy required to increase one manager's salary by 5 percent and another's by 25 percent—they simply do not trust their judgment sufficiently to perform this courageous act. To have a successful compensation plan, managers must be willing to grant widely differentiated increases. As previously stated, this in turn requires that a determined effort be made to reach a genuine understanding between the manager and the managed about the performance level expected.

The second problem in matching increases to performance is that compensation schemes are seldom designed to allow for wide differentials. They are, in fact, often designed to *prevent* differentials by specifying both the amount of increase that may be given and by establishing the upper salary limit of each position. Such plans are intended to provide for the orderly progression of the average performer and therefore fail to accommodate the outstanding performer. Their rigidity derives from the erroneous belief that the established salary range represents "what the job is worth" and that the company cannot afford to pay more for that particular job. The reality of the situation may very well be otherwise in the case of the outstanding performer, as has already been discussed.

In order to make salary administration a fully productive force for corporate improvement, the SITF may find that a broader and somewhat different concept of salary progression is needed. For example, "job value" may be considered as only generally determined by the nature of the duties and responsibilities of the impersonally described position. Value would be more specifically determined by the individual who is performing the duty. Under this concept, the upper limits of the value of a given position are not fixed but may vary, decrease, and increase according to the capabilities of the incumbent executive. This broader concept of compensation requires that it be placed on a more personal and individual basis. Further, it requires that compensation for an individual be viewed from the perspective of his entire career rather than at a single point in that career. From this perspective, the manager's compensation is as much a matter of rate of progress as it is a matter of the absolute amount. It may be more appropriate to assess managers in terms of their own personal rate of development and to assign them to a corresponding rate of salary progression which they maintain as long as that rate of progress is maintained.

At first, this approach might seem to destroy the value of a systematic salary plan; but for most managers—the poor, the average, and the average good—the career path concept for compensation will not conflict with a salary framework which has been well designed. It contrasts with the system of allowing an individual manager's level of compensation to be arbitrarily fixed by the upper and lower limits of a salary box associated with the job he happens to hold at a particular time. The managers who will be affected and for whom it is most needed are the outstanding managers who are moving fast and who must be kept moving if they are to reach the high-level positions they are capable of handling in a reasonably short period. These managers must be given special attention, and, if necessary, allowed to follow a progression that is outside the normal framework. This means that the salary should be established for these managers as a rate of salary progression. For example, if one of the potential career peak levels has a salary expectation of $60,000, the beginning management trainee salary is $10,000, and the expected time to reach the career peak is 20 years, the career compensation path for all members of the group with this potential is one in which salary increases annually at a compound rate of 10 percent. The salary level a member of this group could expect at any point in his career might be illustrated in graphic or tabular form and published along with data for other categories of progression. This would be a better guide to the compensation level of such executives than the impersonal evaluation of the position to which they happened to be assigned at a particular time. On the other hand, the salary ranges assigned to positions should not be completely ignored. If a particular executive is continually being paid more than the maximum level for the job to which he is assigned, this may be an indication that he is not as good as he is supposed to be. Or perhaps he is not being developed fast enough for a more responsible position. When a career path is used for identifying high-talent managers, their exceptional salaries should not be treated as a violation of normal practice and kept secret, but should be treated openly and accepted as part of the normal procedure. Making rates of progress known rather than actual individual salaries will spur competition.

CONCLUSION

The traditional concept of establishing salary levels based on an impersonal view of job worth should be broadened to include the concept of personal career level; this provides guidelines for the "rate of climb" according to the executive's rank in quality of management. For salary purposes, individuals may be identified with specific rates of climb. For example, salaries of the highest grade of managers (perhaps the top 5 percent) might follow a 15 percent compound curve; the lowest retainable managers, a 5 percent compound curve; and others some intermediate rate. The individual's rate of climb may of course change from time to time according to his performance, and he may progress from one career path to another.

In the final analysis, if the audit of a corporate compensation package is to be complete the SITF must venture into yet another important area–utilization of all resources, both human and financial. This area is all-encompassing; it touches upon every aspect of the corporation. With respect to compensation, it is the process of matching financial with human resources.

5

Concept audit of resource allocation and management

Corporations may have two distinctly different types of strategies concerning their resources. If its resources are so abundant that they offer a competitive advantage, resource management will involve strategies to capitalize aggressively upon this advantage. If resources are so scarce that they limit the company's ability to grow, then strategies will necessarily deal with making available resources as productive as possible.

In any given corporation the SITF will find both kinds of strategy and will want to examine the concepts underlying their execution. In the case of strategies designed to capitalize on plentiful resources, underlying concepts usually involve marketing or some outward reaching of the corporation; the SITF may have to range over a wide area in order to pin these concepts down. In the case of limited resources, the primary question is how to allocate what is available to the most productive uses—a question to which there are several very specific conceptual answers. The manner in which the SITF should deal with this group of concepts is covered in this chapter.

Attitudes toward management of resources

Do managers manage operations instead of resources?
Are managers willing to eliminate inefficient resource users?

In all areas of its corporate concept audit the SITF must deal with attitudinal questions; the area of management of resources certainly is no exception to this rule. Before detailed examination of the related concepts is attempted, the SITF must determine whether management has the basic philosophy or frame of mind that is a prerequisite to effective management of resources.

Subtle differences in attitude can make a major difference in approach and results. First, managers must realize that the management of resources takes priority over the management of operations. A highly productive user of resources must take precedence over an efficient but less productive operation. It is self-defeating to improve the efficiency of an operation at the expense of a competing user capable of providing greater leverage from the same resources.

This philosophy ultimately leads to a conclusion that is psychologically difficult for some managers to accept or carry through—that it may be necessary to eliminate a resource user. Resource users can be products, divisions, customers, managers, or anything to which resources are allocated. Users are in competition for resources and should receive or be denied them according to how productively they use them. For one reason or another, however, a manager is often reluctant to eliminate a resource user. He may feel that such an excision implies admission of a mistake and would rather justify by improving than correct by radical removal. Or he may prefer to think of himself as a builder and conservator rather than as a hatchet man. But whatever his reasons or basic attitudes, the manager must have available the appropriate kind of information if he is truly to manage resources.

It is in the area of information concepts that the SITF can make its most concrete evaluations concerning management of resources. At first glance it may seem that many of the concepts recommended for review are so obvious as to require no mention or special treatment from the SITF. The members may, however, be surprised to find that not only is the application of these concepts often misunderstood, but that such applications are often in direct conflict with concepts deeply entrenched in the financial and accounting policies of less progressive companies. This occurs because the information required to evaluate the productivity of resource users requires a rigorous mode of analysis which is radically different from the approach taken by many traditional financial and accounting procedures. Once again, the problem comes back to a basic difference in point of view. Some of the more significant of these differences in emphasis include:

– An attempt to account for all costs as opposed to truly identifying sources of profit.
– An interest in accounting for all financial resources in total as opposed to identifying how they are allocated among users.
– A need to treat costs in a rigid, static, and predetermined manner as opposed to the more dynamic fashion in which they actually behave.

The impact these differences have on the management of resources becomes clear as the SITF examines some of the more detailed concepts involved.

Limiting resources

What resources limit the corporation's achievement of its goals?

For most companies the most apparent limiting resource is financial; certainly, few companies have unlimited funds. The SITF should look beyond financial limitations, however, to see if the scope of thinking about resources is sufficiently broad. The determination of the limiting resource should be approached from the perspective of where the real limitations arise. The answers may include, for example, management or technical talent, raw materials (mining companies), floor space (retailing), or production capacity.

Limiting resources may change from time to time and the corporation should keep constantly aware of their nature. Regardless of what resources are considered limiting, the concepts behind their proper management are the same except that information will usually not be readily available for nonfinancial resources, even though it could certainly become so.

The productivity of resource users

Have all resource users been identified?
Has the productivity of resource users been measured?

Since the basic task of resource management is to assign resources to their most productive uses, measurement of productivity is the first concept the SITF must apply once it has determined the extent to which limiting resources have been identified. The most direct approach for doing this is a misleadingly simple ratio expressing the rate of profitability per unit of resource used:

$$\frac{\text{Direct profit contribution (DPC)}}{\text{Resources Used}}$$

The SITF will very quickly find that an attempt to measure and maximize this ratio can lead to concepts radically different from those traditionally used.

The first area the SITF should examine is the concepts which have been adopted concerning the identity of resource users. It is useful, in this regard, to think of resources as being assigned to profit sources. Profit sources, in turn, may be thought of as the smallest income-producing, resource-using elements which may, individually and in various combinations, be subject to the management action of *elimination.* This would, of course, include individual products, product lines, customers, geographic territories, departments, plants, divisions, and even individual managers who have profit responsibility.

The SITF will quickly see that profit sources, when thought of in this manner, consist of "families" of profit sources which cut across the company in different dimensions, forming a profit contribution matrix. The central concept about profit sources is that they represent discrete units of the manager's control, units about which decisions concerning the allocation of resources should be made. The SITF should satisfy itself that the identification of resource users (profit sources) has been accomplished in a sufficiently broad manner and then go on to the concepts concerning the rate of profitability ratio.

Direct profit contribution (DPC)

Has direct profit contribution been established on a stand-alone basis for each profit source?

The numerator of the resource productivity measure (the direct profit contributed by the profit source) is calculated in a very special manner. Since the manager must be willing to consider eliminating the profit source, he should consider profit contribution to be the diminution in total profit that would occur if the profit source were actually eliminated. This is somewhat more complicated than it first appears.

First of all, there is a tendency in accounting systems to allocate costs downward so that cost and profit figures for individual profit sources do not stand alone. That is, costs incurred independently of the profit source are nevertheless assigned and attached to it in some way. The manager, therefore, has difficulty in judging the real economic impact of the profit source on the company. For example, a product with a selling price of $2.00 and an indicated cost of $1.60 does not really increase profit by $.40 per unit. To find out exactly how much profit it does produce, the manager must know those costs which were allocated to it although not generated by it. If the $1.60 cost included, for example, an allocation of $.60 of the costs of plant depreciation, manager salaries, and other fixed costs, the real impact of that product is to increase net profit by $1.00, not $.40 for each unit sold.

This sort of allocation is brought about by a perspective which can best be described as "from the top down." That is, the cost of managers and other fixed costs incurred at the "higher" levels are allocated downward through the organization until they are finally spread over the smallest income-producing unit—usually a product. The SITF will find that the opposite or a "bottom up" perspective is much more useful in the management of resources.

At the product level certain costs, such as labor and materials, are incurred specifically for the product. As you move up in the organization to the department level, the costs are incurred on a broader and broader base. The cost incurred at the department level cannot be associated uniquely with individual products; and costs incurred at the corporate level cannot be associated with individual departments. This line of distinction is precisely what the cost structure ought to be designed to show because it is only from this basis that the manager can evaluate the "eliminate" decision before him and make the proper allocation of resources.

The SITF must be careful in analyzing the use of this concept to insure that it is applied correctly. It is not enough, for example, to accept an expense as a "department" expense simply because it is so classified on the company's chart of accounts. The real test lies in determining what the expense is *truly* associated with, and this is revealed by analysis of *what would have to be eliminated in order to make it possible to eliminate the expense.* A portion of direct labor would be eliminated if a product were eliminated; a product specialist would be eliminated if a product line were eliminated; and a foreman would be eliminated if a department were eliminated. Until costs are in this manner associated at the proper level with profit sources, it will not be possible to measure profit contribution.

Cost behavior

Is the behavior of each cost understood in relation to profit sources?

It is necessary to know if costs are associated with a profit source in such a manner as to be eliminable if the profit source is eliminated. Actually, a further refinement in knowledge about cost behavior is required. How are costs affected by changes in the volume of the profit source? Some costs, such as raw materials, will vary in direct proportion to volume. Others, such as indirect labor, may vary slightly but not proportionately with changes in volume. Still others, such as supervision, may not vary at all, at least until the changes become quite large; and then they may alter abruptly. Because of these variations in cost relationships, direct profit contribution is different at different rates of activity. The SITF should examine the concepts used to state profit source costs to determine that this changing relationship is understood.

Moving to the numerator of the ratio, the SITF will usually find that resources are associated with profit sources only in the grossest way. A company will ordinarily know its total financial investment in a plant or division and regularly determine and report return on investment. Few companies, however, will take the trouble to determine how much of their investment is incrementally associated with a particular product in a multiproduct operation, although without this determination it is obviously not possible to measure resource productivity.

Financial resources have the same characteristics of variability as costs. A capital investment in a manufacturing plant is fixed, and once made is not available for other alternative investments. When comparing the *capital* productivity (not capacity productivity), the capital resources associated with the product should not include the fixed-plant investment, but should include any capital investment which would be directly affected by that product. This would include, for example, the investment required in its inventory and its accounts receivable as well as other effects on cash requirements. If the limiting resource being studied was production capacity rather than financial capacity, then it would be appropriate to determine profit contribution on the basis of capacity used, provided that there is an alternative use of that capacity. In fact, the SITF should apply this important rule to any analysis of resource productivity. The resources associated with a profit source in analyzing productivity should include only those which *could be released for other uses.* There is very little point, for example, in calculating resource productivity for the total investment in a special-purpose machine that can make only one product *after* the investment has already been made, even though the capital account will show an unamortized investment. The cash involved is gone and is simply not available for other alternatives. The fact that some investments are recoverable or convertible to other uses and some are not has an important implication in making investment decisions. The SITF may wish to examine whether a corporation's investment criteria, in terms of return on investment, adequately recognize the different characteristics of these risks.

Other solutions to problems of resource management

Is resource velocity maximized?
Is pricing policy geared to resource productivity?

The SITF will also want to consider approaches to resource management other than reallocation. The first of these is a direct approach to improving the *rate* of productivity. Obviously, if the efficiency with which a profit source uses a resource can be improved, this should be done. The SITF should remember that *rate* implies *velocity;* the faster resources are turned over, the greater is their productivity. This is a particularly fruitful line of attack where financial resources are invested in inventory, since there are many ways in which inventory management can be improved.

Another way productivity can possibly be improved is through pricing policy. Here is the source of another potential conflict with the traditional accounting approach. The SITF will usually find that the "top down" allocating approach tends to maximize *profit per unit sold,* whereas the entire theme has been that resource management involves maximizing profit per unit of resource used.

These two approaches result in different pricing policies. In the first, price is set at some point above the total of direct and allocated costs on the theory that some portion of allocated costs and profit must be recovered from the sale of each product. Under this theory, selling price cannot be less than the total of direct and allocated cost. Under the resource productivity concept, however, price is established so that

Profit contribution per unit x Total number of units

is a maximum. It can be shown that except in very rare cases this formula will maximize return on a resource. It also means that selling price per unit can theoretically be at any level above direct costs but not necessarily enough to cover the allocated costs. This is because, as price changes, market demand and volume sold may also change. And total profit is a function of both volume and unit profit contribution.

In the previous example of a product with a total direct and allocated cost of $1.60, the selling price may have been set according to a pricing policy which states that "prices will be set to recover all allocated fixed costs plus a 20 percent (on selling price) gross profit." At the $2.00 price, the DPC has already been indicated to be $1.00. To make a decision on the *most profitable* price, it is necessary to judge the effect of price on volume. If, for example, anticipated volume is 20,000 units at $2.00, the contribution is $20,000. Total profit could be increased by decreasing price to $1.50 (a $.50 DPC) if the resulting volume would thus be increased to 50,000 units. Even though the selling price is less than the indicated direct and allocated cost of $1.60, total DPC would be increased to $25,000.

It has already been mentioned that different profit source families cut across the company in different dimensions and thus overlap.

For example, a company sells two product lines, typewriters and calculators, in two states, Oklahoma and Texas. This is a two-family (territory and product) profit source matrix with four primary profit sources: typewriters, calculators, Oklahoma, and Texas, with four subcategories as shown in the matrix.

Profit source matrix

	Product lines		
Territories	*Typewriters*	*Calculators*	*Total*
Oklahoma	Oklahoma Typewriter DPC	Oklahoma Calculator DPC	X X
Texas	Texas Typewriter DPC	Texas Calculator DPC	X X
Total	X X	X X	X X

Typewriters make a direct profit contribution comprised of the contribution from sales in Oklahoma and Texas. When profit contribution shown in this matrix is calculated on a "stand alone" basis, the figures inside the matrix may be quite meaningful. The space, for example, can be accurately described as the profit contribution of typewriters to Oklahoma or vice versa. This is meaningful because stand-alone profit contribution is defined as the net result of having that product in that territory unclouded by allocation of costs from other sources. The insight applies to considerations of increasing volume just as effectively as it does to the question of complete elimination.

The two-dimension matrix is simpler than the typical company situation which includes other families of profit sources such as managers or customer groups coming together to produce a four-dimension or even more complex matrix. Allocating costs to profit sources prohibits such matrices from being meaningful because the figures inside the matrix do not directly reveal exactly what would happen if particular items were "lifted out" or removed. Allocation of fixed costs forces a choice of just which family of profit sources will be reported at a particular time. This is a handicap in gaining a full understanding of just how profit is produced in a company and in making the necessary decisions concerning the allocation of limiting resources to maximize profit.

The profit source matrix

Are the company's profit sources understood and treated as a total structure?

The SITF investigation has been concerned with viewing individual profit sources and evaluating the relative effectiveness with which they utilize resources. Once a company has adopted the appropriate position on costs and decision-making posture, it is then in a position to take a broader and more meaningful view of the total profit structure of the company.

Profit structure is comprised of the collection of all individual profit sources which exist within the company. The structure, as a total entity, has significance for two reasons. First, individual profit sources within the structure have a special relationship to each other, and the manner in which the individual profit sources are grouped can affect the company's overall profit-making ability.

The other aspect of the profit structure is the hierarchical arrangement of cost buildup and profit contribution. The "bottom up" perspective is needed in cost buildup. This is because the nature and behavior of costs at each level are very different and consequently profit needs to be thought of as being generated differentially at each level. The hierarchical manner in which costs and profits are generated is illustrated in the following matrix showing only one family of profit sources (products) with two products in each of two product lines.

	Line A			*Line B*			
	Product			*Product*			*Grand Total*
	1	2	*Total A*	1	2	*Total B*	
Sales	100	150	250	200	100	300	550
Less: Direct costs	60	50	110	120	50	170	280
Product profit contribution	40	100	140	80	50	130	270
Less: Cost of product-line manager	–	–	40	–	–	60	100
Product-line contribution	–	–	100	–	–	70	170
Less: Corporate expense	–	–	–	–	–	–	100
Net Profit	–	–	–	–	–	–	70

This matrix shows a distinctly different profit contribution at each level, beginning at the product level where contribution is, of course, largest. At each higher level, profit contribution is diminished by deducting the expenses at that level until finally corporate level expenses are deducted to arrive at net profit. It will also be seen that profit-planning decisions are different at each level. At the product level, profit contribution is determined by the cost-price-volume relationship–how many units at what unit profit contribution. At the product line (department level) it is a question of how many products (profit sources) should be under one manager or, put another way, what is the most appropriate grouping of products.

In more complex structures, when considering all the feasible alternatives that are possible in the design of the company's profit structure, questions arise such as what marketing staff, advertising, or other support functions make the best (most profitable) grouping and arrangement of profit sources. The profit matrix with standalone profit contribution data presents profit sources somewhat in the fashion of building blocks which may be put together in the most appropriate form.

So far, the discussion of the profit source matrix has mentioned only profit contribution. A mirror image of this matrix, showing the limiting resources used by each profit source, is also needed in order to provide information on rate of productivity. The productivity ratio is then obtained by dividing the profit contribution matrix by the resource assignment matrix.

Information reporting

How much information on profit contribution and resource productivity is needed?

The SITF must consider the very practical question of how far the company should go in analyzing and reporting profit contribution and resource data. The answer depends partly on management's willingness to follow the disciplined approach required by a full-blown system. It also depends to some extent on the ultimate significance of the data collected. The SITF can judge this significance by determining the volatility of costs between time periods and the degree to which profit contribution is differentiated among profit sources.

For most companies, the first step would at least be informative and worth taking. This involves an analysis of cost and resource behavior and an initial determination of the inherent rate of profit contribution for individual profit sources on a one-time basis, much like a snapshot. This information reveals "normal" expectations of individual profit sources as well as the distribution of profit contributions among sources. On the basis of this information, a decision could be made as to whether a more extensive information-gathering study should be pursued. An example will serve to show the type of information such a study can reveal.

A department store chain made a detailed study of product class and departmental profitability in their stores. (A class is a distinct type of merchandise such as living room furniture, ladies' sportswear, or men's dress shirts.) The objective was to devise a practical and economically feasible measure of the direct profit contribution of each class and each department. They measured profitability on each merchandise class in three different ways.

First, they measured DPC per unit of sales and in total for the year. Next, they measured DPC per dollar invested in each product class. Investment in inventory and credit sales were included in the measure. Finally, they measured DPC per square foot of floor space devoted to each class.

The results of the study were quite revealing. These measures gave a vastly different picture of profitability from the traditional gross margin plus discount used in the department store industry. They clearly suggested that some changes in merchandise policy would increase departmental return, simply because some classes used resources so poorly.

The accompanying table is representative of some of the actual data collected during the study. It illustrates the differences found between the traditional gross margin plus discount measure and DPC data. Significantly, various methods gave different results—both in rank of profitability and in order of magnitude. Depending upon which resources are considered most critical, the merchandising and pricing policies will be set up differently under the guidance of these figures.

Under gross margin plus discount, the profitability of the highest class, Class A, is 52 percent and that of the lowest, Class F is 33 percent. This means that Class A is only 1½ times better than Class F. Under DPC per $ of sales, Class A contributes 39 percent or 2½ times more than Class F's 14 percent to sales. Under DPC per square foot, Class A is still the highest, with Class B the lowest. Class A contributes $102 per square foot per year, which is 10 times better than Class B's $10. Under DPC per $ invested, the class rank changes. Class D is the highest, contributing $6.18 or 22 times more than the lowest, Class F's $0.28. Cash in Class D is 30 times more

Class profitability indices

	Profitability as measured by traditional department store method		*Profitability as measured by direct profit contribution*		*Productivity by type of resource for which classes are competing.*			
					Floor space		*Financial*	
*Merchandise class**	*Gross margin + discount*	*Rank*	*DPC per $ Sales*	*Rank*	*DPC per sq. ft.*	*Rank*	*DPC per $ invested*	*Rank*
A	52.36%	1	39.93%	1	$102.17	1	$4.62	2
B	48.79	2	30.59	4	10.97	6	3.56	3
C	48.68	3	31.60	3	25.44	4	1.75	4
D	48.32	4	38.00	2	75.95	2	6.18	1
E	44.80	5	26.73	5	45.77	3	1.70	5
F	33.46	6	14.96	6	12.86	5	.28	6

*Merchandise class refers to distinct types of merchanidse assigned to a particular buyer, i.e., living room furniture, women's sportswear, and men's dress shirts.

productive than cash invested in Class F. It does not matter that the store cannot actually eliminate Class F. The buyers were very much influenced by facts like these.

If profit contribution is highly differentiated as well as volatile, the company may opt for an extensive program. Such a program could include:

- –Normal profit contribution expected from each profit source.
- –Dynamic cost data which can be used to predict cost and profit data under various conditions of volume and product mix.
- –A system for reporting actual cost and profit contribution data for each profit source on a regular basis.

The reporting system referred to could vary from a relatively simple manual system to a highly detailed and complicated computer-based system. The general concept of reporting profit contribution in a meaningful way for an entire profit structure is illustrated in the attached table. This table is a three-dimension profit contribution matrix using the profit source families of product line, territory, and customer group. Costs are associated in this report with level and profit source family for which they are incurred. Direct profit contribution is, therefore, on a stand-alone basis. Three-dimension reports are about as complicated as a useful report can be, and if other profit sources are worth considering the SITF should probably recommend additional reports. The profit contribution matrix report may seem to be rather complicated and it is. However, if a company has several families of significant profit sources it has an inherently complicated situation to begin with; and the reporting of profit contribution makes for a less rather than a more complicated situation. Unless the managers of a corporation have a thorough understanding of its profit structure, they cannot grasp the corporation as a total profit-making organization.

CONCLUSIONS

The management of resources is a central issue for the SITF. The organization structure may be well designed, managers may be well motivated, and the corporation may operate efficiently, but unless limiting resources are allocated to their most productive uses, the

Three-dimension matrix of profit contribution by profit source

	Product line 1			*Product line 2*			*Sum of profit contribution*			
	Product 11	*Product 12*	*Sum of territory contribution to Product Line 1*	*Product 21*	*Product 22*	*Sum of territory contribution to Product Line 2*	*Territory M*	*Territory N*	*Customer group X*	*Customer group Y*
Customer Group X										
Territory M	x x	x x	x x	x x	x x	x x	x x			
Territory N	x x	x x	x x	x x	x x	x x		x x		
Sum of Profit Contribution for Group X	x x	x x	x x	x x	x x	x x			x x	
Customer Group Y										
Territory M	x x	x x	x x	x x	x x	x x	x x			
Territory N	x x	x x	x x	x x	x x	x x		x x		
Sum of Profit Contribution for Group Y	x x	x x	x x	x x	x x	x x				x x
Sum of Profit Source Contribution	x x	x x	x x	x x	x x	x x	x x	x x	x x	x x
Less Costs Associated with Profit Source	x x	x x	x x	x x	x x	x x	x x	x x	x x	x x
Total Profit Contribution of Profit Source	x x	x x	x x	x x	x x	x x	x x	x x	x x	x x

corporation can never approach its maximum effectiveness. The SITF will, therefore, pay careful attention to the manner in which resources are allocated and the way in which their productivity is measured. This is a vital part of the corporate design which the SITF must evaluate as a total pattern.

6

Concept audit of the total corporation

The SITF's most important job is to examine the corporation as a total entity and to make judgments about its basic concepts from a global perspective. This requires not only that SITF members be incisive in evaluating the individual elements in relation to the total corporation, but also that they evaluate the corporation in relation to its total situation.

As the SITF goes about its work of auditing the concepts behind individual elements such as organization structure, managers, and management of resources, it will acquire a "feel" for the total fitness of the corporation. It needs to do more, however, than merely collect overall impressions as it goes along and add them up at the end. It should pay special attention to several factors which can be viewed properly only from the perspective of the total corporation.

The central idea the SITF must examine is the corporation's relationship with its environment. The corporation exists in a general environment and must cope with the environment by acting or reacting. Whether it continues to exist often depends not only on how efficiently it relates to its environment but also on the posture it adopts toward certain exterior groups or pressures.

In the past, corporate success has been largely a factor of technology, power, and ability to assess a market, but in the future success may also depend on the corporation's willingness to respond to social pressures. Popular movements concerned with consumerism, social and environmental responsibility, and enrichment of human lives may be regarded by some people as surface developments, but there is evidence that they are increasing in force. It seems very probable that corporations are going to be shaped by these forces, whether they like it or not. The SITF should consider not only the corporation's stance toward such issues, but also whether or not that stance has its basis in adequate knowledge.

Beyond the corporation's position on social issues, its general state of readiness to change and to adapt to environmental conditions should also be determined by the SITF. Because of the acceleration in rate of change in the world at large, corporate ability to adapt is becoming a critical characteristic that must be consciously built into the corporation's design. For this it must maintain a receptivity to new knowledge and new techniques.

In the course of its audit, the SITF will have pinpointed many opportunities for improving the design of the corporation. Its work is not complete, however, until it decides which improvements should be made, at what rate, and in what order. Each corporation has its own "appropriate" rate of change, depending on the urgency of its needs and also on its *capacity* for change. The SITF must present its recommendations with full consideration given to these factors as they exist in the total corporation. This chapter covers conceptual areas pertaining to the total corporation—the corporation's posture in its environment, its ability to adapt and redesign itself, and its capacity for change.

The corporate posture in its environment

What is the corporate posture on the new forces at work in its environment?

Has this position been assumed on the basis of an honest consideration of the factors involved?

What is the appropriate measure of the performance of the corporation?

The social issues with which the corporation must deal are broadly defined by three terms: consumerism: social or environmental responsibility, and quality of work. In all three categories the SITF must determine if the corporation has taken its position on the basis of real knowledge of the issues or merely by default—by simply refusing to acknowledge the issues.

The basic question regarding consumerism is, "how much responsibility does the company feel toward its customers?" In order to clarify this issue, we must realize that the starting point for the enlightened company is how much responsibility the company should assume above and beyond that required to maintain public acceptance. Conceptually, this is a very simple issue because, up to this minimum point, it is the company's welfare that is at stake. Many companies facing this issue honestly today will decide to assume no additional responsibility. Difficult as the practical application of this choice may be, the matter is simplified if the issue is clarified in the beginning. If a corporation decides to assume responsibility beyond the minimum point, it must carefully spell out the terms of the responsibility so that it can be administered consistently throughout the company.

Social responsibility is an issue covering a broad range of subjects from fair treatment of minority groups to protection of the environment. Here again, honesty is required on the part of the policy-making executives if subsequent action is to hit the mark. Business policy makers will have to address these questions concerning "social responsibility" continually during the next decade. Whether or not they feel an inner conviction that their corporation should accept social responsibilities, they will not be able to ignore all of the outside demands.

At a very minimum, policy makers must adopt the strategy of doing the least acceptable amount of "good works," responding to public attitudes to the degree necessary to maintain their public image. This is said not out of cynicism but out of the realization that the values of a corporation are the values of its policy makers. It is not the business of the SITF to take a position (unless its members also happen to be the company's policy makers), but rather to clarify the nature of values and to judge how well the operations accord with them.

Some policy-making executives nowadays feel a genuine social responsibility. These executives are likely to take the view that some of the corporation's profits *should* be spent in relieving human misery—that a corporation's property and power not only give it certain rights but also create certain obligations to protect and preserve the environment for all those to come in the future.

Thus far no commonly accepted method has been developed for measuring the degree to which a company is meeting its social responsibility. Improvements in the quality of life cannot be measured precisely, if at all. If a company acts from public relations motives, the "right" amount is the amount acceptable to the public. If it acts because of its value system, the right amount is best determined by its own sense of what is appropriate.

The third group of special concerns is popularly referred to by such terms as self-actualization, participative management, and job enrichment or quality of work. Many believe that the American worker (and perhaps the worker of the world) is bored with his life and job, and that this is a major social problem of our time. The implication is that most of the responsibility for doing something about it rests with the corporation. The SITF and the policy-making, value-setting executives should realize that there is another view on this subject which may be more beneficial to the thinking manager. The humanitarian approach to employee relations is generally based on an attitude of paternalism. This is essentially a sentimental or selfish attitude and does not support a feeling of self-respect among employees. In contrast, a philosophy sometimes referred to as humanism places ultimate priority on human dignity and human worth. Men who hold this philosophy have a deep interest in the human condition and judge their own actions on the basis of their impact on other human beings involved. They believe in the primary importance of creating opportunities for individuals to develop their full potential. Managers having the humanist view are usually interested in making work more fulfilling, but they are also interested in making work more productive because they are managers. The two aims are neither contradictory nor complementary. They are simply two different specifications that can be applied at the same time to improve the total quality of work—that is, to make it better from the point of view of both the employee and of the corporation.

The SITF should be interested in the corporate attitude toward productivity. There are very few companies that can afford either a humanitarian (anti-efficiency) or an indifferent attitude toward increasing productivity. Even though a company's economic situation may not require increased productivity at present, the situation can change overnight. Many companies have found after years of being unconcerned about the productivity of their employees, their capital, or other resources, that a sudden need to become more productive was difficult to satisfy. As the rate of technological change increases, the probability that a company will be forced to attend to productivity increases along with it.

Productivity has a humanistic side, however. The poverty and general lack of self-respect found among many American Indians on reservations have been largely eliminated among the Pueblo Indians. As industry of various types has come into their area, the Pueblo Indians have become productive workers. Their work is not necessarily interesting or challenging, but it has increased the Indians' self-respect.

The SITF must also consider ways of measuring the quality of work. Productivity can be measured in a number of ways: output per manhour, output per dollar invested, and the like. But no single measure is complete in itself; and measurement is infinitely more difficult where human self-actualization is involved. Probably no one is wise enough to say what self-actualization is. Real self-actualization probably requires greater self-knowledge than most people have, so that it represents only a partially attainable goal at best. The SITF may, therefore, find it impossible to measure what the corporation achieves in the way of self-actualization for its employees. This should not, of course, be a reason for abandoning the concept if it is otherwise applicable.

The corporation's position relative to social and environmental responsibilities may be determined by a desire to be responsible or by a need to acknowledge social pressures. Its position relative to its willingness to change, however, is required by a changing environment to which it must adapt if it is to survive.

The corporation's ability to adapt to its environment by changing its design

Has responsibility for corporate design been assigned and accepted?

Have major corporate-wide systems been identified and dealt with as systems?

Have systems engineering approaches been used to improve corporate-wide systems?

Is the corporation keeping up with the development of knowledge?

Is the corporation using the latest management methods and tools to its advantage?

Does the corporation conduct research to improve its knowledge about its own functioning?

Are performance standards set from a total corporate point of view?

Corporate survival is an appropriate subject for the SITF. The specific capabilities this requires will be unique to each corporation. But the location of some generalized capabilities that apply to most corporate situations should be a helpful start. One of the first and most obvious things to consider is the responsibility for corporate design. A provision should be made to carry on this work on a continuous basis after the SITF finishes its concept audit.

It is appropriate to think of an effort devoted solely to the design of the total corporation. For the small company, a portion of the chief executive's time should be devoted to thinking about the overall shape of his company and how it could be made more effective. For the large corporation, a full-fledged department might be dedicated to corporate design. Regardless of the size of the effort, its essence is to deal more broadly with the corporate form than do the departments currently concerned with corporate systems, management information systems, organizational development, or long-range planning.

A corporate design department should be primarily concerned with basic changes that will increase the corporation's capabilities for meeting challenges, improving and clarifying concepts and systems, and improving methods of problem solving. The department would not be concerned with the performance of individuals or with day-to-day problems. In dealing with the structure of the corporation, however, it would relate to and be potentially concerned with all aspects of the corporation. To clarify the role of a department of corporate design so that it will not be confused with planning or other staff groups such as organizational or systems specialists, we might say that in any given case the function of corporate design might overlap with the functions of other departments. Its role would be distinguished, however, by the breadth of its scope and the depth of its probing—by a difference in primary responsibility. Anticipating long-range problems and prescribing the basic changes required to meet them, and developing and refining key concepts of organizational functioning, would be its general purposes. It would design the method of problem solving, define the underlying structure of the corporation, and develop and store basic knowledge required for strategy and planning.

Management science and other developments now make it possible for a corporate design department to work on a very comprehensive basis. Computers, along with behavioral science and systems engineering, make it possible to articulate, understand, and solve management problems as never before. The success of corporate design is largely dependent upon expressing key concepts precisely and vigorously; when couched in imprecise or generalized language, they shed little light on concrete situations. The corporate scientist, like an engineer, chemist, physician, or psychologist, must render the results of analytic work in a concrete and definite manner. Corporate design must be able to translate top-level thinking into a plan for action, and also to translate the corporate results stemming from management inputs into a form that management can use.

In addition to verbal logic, corporate design has two very powerful tools with which to express and improve concepts more effectively. These tools are mathematical models and systems engineering, and they are useful because they are precise and because they make it possible to predict results of various decisions and conditions. Several decades ago, before these technological advances, the concept of corporate design would have been improbable. Managers are now challenged to assimilate this knowledge and to develop better concepts of total organization. Today, corporate design as a separate, identifiable, and somewhat innovative department, is a viable concept.

One of the most important requirements for keeping the corporation viable is a store of knowledge and self-understanding. Most corporate research is oriented toward products, processes, or markets. Research on the corporation should be aimed at discovering the dynamic relationships among corporate elements. That is, it should find a means of predicting the effect of other functions or actions taken in support of a given function. It should find a means of predicting the effect, throughout the company, of specified units of input. It should be able to judge the relative merits or demerits of alternative decisions, estimate the impact on operations of uncertain events, and specify changes or actions necessary to achieve a desired result. It should also provide a record of past actions and of results derived from those actions. While managers do these things more or less intuitively, corporate design, as a department solely dedicated to keeping abreast of them, will be able to do so in a more organized, coordinated, and efficient manner. This will lead to an improved corporate ability to make decisions, formulate strategy, and control operations. The corporate design department should be thought of as the center of conceptual thinking for the entire corporation.

There is a tendency in management literature to regard performance standards as representing a high level of performance and thus to associate such standards with motivation for high performance. A more useful concept of standards is to assume that they express merely a *satisfactory* or *necessary* level of performance. In this view, motivation to higher levels of performance should be left to goal-setting and other forms of incentive. For corporate purposes, then, performance standards are the level of performance required individually or collectively for the corporation to meet its goals. Standards should be established with reference to the corporate goals rather than with reference to what represents satisfactory individual performance. The establishment of corporate standards should, therefore, be a task of the corporate design department and should provide a floor or a base under all other standards.

Most corporate standards are obvious and rather gross: for example, "a division must make x percent return on its investment or be shut down." At this point the contribution made by corporate design is in clarifying obscure factors and refining and expressing critical relationships. Corporate design begins with corporate goals for profit or growth and then translates them into terms appropriate for individual functions or units. The standards will normally be in terms of units of output per unit of input, or in terms of the relationship one factor must bear to another. The standards may be derived from internal or external circumstances. Corporate standards are the base line for the expression of all other individual standards. Individuals or departments may set their own standards based upon desired levels of competence, but, collectively, these standards must equal or be higher than the corporate standards. On the other hand, corporate design will indirectly influence the level of individual standards by revealing through its analysis the full profit-making potential of the corporation, thus elevating the level of corporate goals. For example, corporate design may examine the rate of improvement in production technology in the industry and translate this into product costs which must be achieved to maintain a competitive position. Or it may establish the unit cost which must be achieved to meet a certain return on investment.

IDENTIFYING AND IMPROVING MAJOR CORPORATE SYSTEMS AND SUBSYSTEMS

In order for the corporate design function to attack major corporate design problems from a total corporate perspective, it must have a well-developed concept of systems and how to improve them. Most concepts of a system are narrowly confined to the flow of information and paperwork. Corporate design must be capable of understanding and dealing with more comprehensive systems using mathematical, psychological, engineering, and other analytical techniques. The corporation is a composite of many systems: production, physical, financial, and others. Many are so embedded and interwoven in the activities of the corporation that they are not recognizable as distinct systems. Each corporation has its own set of factors dictating which systems are most critical.

Aside from identifying major corporate systems, the SITF should determine whether or not the corporation is taking a "systems" approach to its own design and improvement. Systems engineering is a relatively new discipline that makes it possible to analyze a series of related events and to understand and control them as a system. One method of seeing that a "system" approach is taken to the affairs of the corporation is to include a systems engineer in the corporate design group. However, the corporate design group can do an effective job of systems engineering without such a specialist if it keeps in mind several important factors. First, it will be helpful to define further what is meant by a system.

In its simplest form, a system can be thought of as "inputs into a process from which come outputs":

Inputs ⟶ Process ⟶ Outputs

Inputs are some form of resource: balance sheet items, talent, knowledge, and information, or perhaps merely an attitude among a group of individuals. *Process* is action or decision-making which converts the input into a different form of resource, the *output.* Stated in a slightly different way, our concept of a system is "the process of converting resources into another, hopefully larger, resource." Under this definition, every major departmental function is an element of one or more systems and should be identified as such if sufficient understanding of the company is to be achieved. Our concept of a system may be expanded from a single process with inputs and outputs to a series of connected events. The output of each event becomes the input (or part of the input) of the succeeding event, for the full length of the chain. We thus enrich our systems concept by thinking of events as the flow of resources through processes which change and enlarge their form and substance.

HOW SYSTEMS ARE IMPROVED ONCE THEY HAVE BEEN DEFINED

Once the important systems—many of which have not previously been recognized as separate and distinct—have been identified, they must be carefully defined and their basic concepts clarified. The next step is to decide what the system is trying to maximize and to make explicit its objectives and constraints. This is a critical test because, if the objectives and constraints are not completely clear, nothing further can be done about improving the system and more time must be spent in its definition. Once the objectives and constraints are well in mind, four basic avenues are open to the improvement of the system: increasing efficiency, improving coordination, increasing velocity of output, and improving system control. *

Improving efficiency

Corporate design should not be concerned with the internal efficiency of involved departments, but, rather, with the inherent efficiency of the overall process being used. We speak here of efficiency in the classical sense of output divided by input. To improve efficiency is to increase the output generated per unit of resource input. In its attempts to improve efficiency, corporate design might recommend a more efficient process in the departments involved or in the arrangement of individual departments comprising the system.

Improving coordination

Coordination of a system influences the performance of constituent elements so that they make the greatest possible contribution to the net results of the total system. This influence may affect the timing or performance of a function or it may limit or extend the function in some way. It is corporate design's responsibility to check the coordination of the units making up the system. This may involve improving the information flow among departments, changing the organizational structure to improve communication channels or enhance accountability, increasing or decreasing the centralization of authority, analyzing the timing requirements among the functions performed by various departments, or developing means of achieving proper balance among opposing objectives.

> The physical distribution system is an example of a system in which constituent units must be carefully balanced. The entire sequence of material flow, beginning with the purchase of raw materials and extending through storage, manufacturing, warehousing, and the delivery of products to customers, should be regarded as a *single system.* The elements of this system include not only the handling, transportation, and purchasing practices for materials, but also where and how they are stored. It thus influences the geographical configuration of the company. As with most systems, the physical distribution system is subject to opposing objectives and, therefore, a proper balance must be sought. There is the need for fast delivery and quick availability necessitating a large investment in inventory and facilities. Investment, transportation, and handling costs are generally reduced if storage and manufacturing locations are more centralized. Corporate design can construct a model which will aid management in reaching an optimum effectiveness. There are certain elements in a system such as this, however, which prevent the final solution from being expressed as a net minimum cost. It may not be wise, for example, to attempt to express the level of service of alternative systems in terms of dollars. It is more practical to express the level of service in terms of the delivery time associated with each level of system cost, and to allow management to select the combination of level of service and system cost which it intuitively feels is optimum. Another function of corporate design in designing the physical distribution system is to find methods which will improve either the level of service or the operating costs. By analyzing each element of the system and its effect upon other elements, corporate design should be able to uncover, define, and articulate to top management the place for important improvements in the design of the system.

Increasing the velocity of output

Systems are the flow of resources through a transformation process; and because the end result of the process is more desirable than the beginning, the faster the process is completed the better. The system will be improved if the velocity of resource flow through the system can be increased. In more practical terms, this means that resources will be "turned" faster, and fewer will be tied up in the process. The relevance of this objective to a resource such as cash is apparent; however, its relevance to non-balance sheet resources such as information may not be so obvious. The importance of these items will be more readily appreciated if one traces them backward through the system of which they are a part. When this is done it is observed that the items go through a process of metamorphosis progressing from balance sheet items to other forms and ultimately become balance sheet resources again. Their velocity through the system determines how long resources will be non-balance sheet items as opposed to being balance sheet items. As a general principle, non-balance sheet resources involve a greater exposure to risk than balance sheet resources because there is always the possibility that they will not survive the cycle.

A look at the financial system will further emphasize and clarify the importance velocity of output has upon a total system. A financial system is the flow of financial resources into uses and back to resources again, hopefully levered by the desired return on investment. The balance sheet is a static picture of this system showing how financial resources (liabilities) are allocated among uses (assets) at any given time. The balance sheet is indispensable to financial management of a company in that it exposes a static picture of a dynamic situation. However, it is not the only type of information management should have. Also needed is the pattern of flow itself. Corporate design contributes to the understanding and definition of this flow in a form useful to management. Traditionally, management of a financial system is influenced by rules handed down from generation to generation. These rules cover parameters of the financial system establishing such things as the limit or ratio of debt to equity and of current assets to current liabilities. While these rules, empirically determined, have provided management with some practical guidance in the control of financial affairs, they are not based upon scientific investigation. Corporate design can conduct scientific investigation in an almost virgin field and improve management's understanding of a financial system. The concept of "system" becomes clearer if we represent its features diagrammatically.

Study of the diagram below reveals several features of the concept that seem worthy of management attention. The diagram shows by directional arrows how resources are allocated among classes which are then committed to operations (manufacturing and marketing). "Operations" is a "multiplier" which takes resources committed to it and converts them to another form of asset–accounts receivable. These are expanded beyond the original amount by the rate of profit.

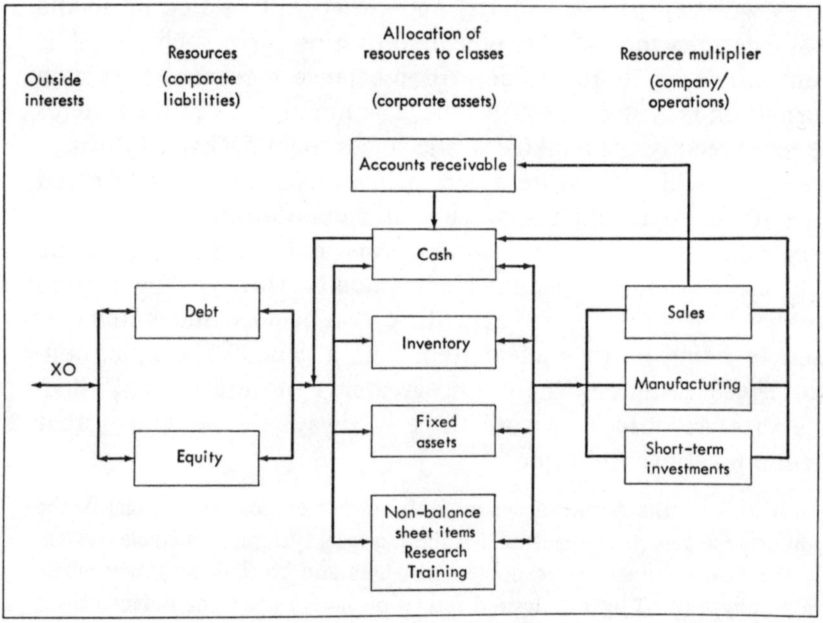

While this diagrammatic approach may be oversimplified, it does have value by virtue of its ability to present the total financial operation as a related system and its ability to suggest some interesting areas of scientific investigation with relation to corporate design. Notice that the flow is circular, or in loops. This suggests that whenever something takes place within any element in the system there is potentially a resulting effect on other elements of the system. If the system is understood as a system, such causes and effects can be understood and predicted. For example, a change in activity in operations not only changes the allocation of resources among resource classes but also changes the total quantity of resources needed. Total resources can be changed by changing either debt or equity. Increasing debt (or decreasing equity) can increase the return on equity, but it also increases the exposure to risk for equity diminution. By increasing understanding of how the magnitude of this risk changes as debt increases, corporate design can greatly enhance management's understanding of a financial system. Another way of viewing the financial system is to recognize that the rate of return on investment is a function of the rate of flow or velocity of the values throughout the "system."

Improving system control

A given system may or may not be susceptible to improvement of its efficiency, rate of resource flow, or coordination. Very few systems exist, however, which cannot benefit from knowledgeable efforts to improve control over their operation. The concept of control itself is often confused. Norbert Wiener's cybernetic concept of control states that systems are "adaptive mechanisms." That is, systems are not only capable of moving toward an objective but also are self-correcting when they fail to progress toward the objective. It is the "self-correcting" feature of a system that represents control. The feature which makes control possible is feedback to the controlling mechanism—feedback of information on how well the system's output is meeting the objectives. The control function determines and points toward the corrections in the input needed to bring output to the ideal level. In most business systems the manager performs the control function, while information systems of various types provide feedback.

The degree of control that can be exercised over a system is influenced by the quality of information contained in the feedback. It is, therefore, in the improvement of quality of feedback information that corporate design must make its contribution to improved system control. There are several ways in which the quality of information can be improved. First, the reliability of predictions of output for a given input can be improved through research. This would be helpful in reducing the manager's uncertainty about what action to take. Second, an early warning system may be designed so that the manager will know in advance that his output is not going to meet the objectives of the system. This requires that corporate design carefully investigate the system and determine what the behavior patterns of its various elements may be predicting. Third, it is sometimes possible to make diagnoses from available information that will point toward the source of a problem and indicate the nature of the corrective action which should be taken. Finally, corporate design should undertake a general study of the system and make a general analysis of what information is needed to control it. Managers responsible for the system will have various levels of insight into the amount and type of information needed to run it, and corporate design should also make its own independent analysis. The quality of such information is improved by research; and research may even determine what information is useful and predictive.

The corporation's ability to change

What is the nature of the changes which the corporation should make?

How rapidly should these changes be made?

Through what instruments or by what methods should the changes be made?

The final act of the SITF will be to prepare a recommendation specifying the changes in corporate configuration it believes are desirable as well as how soon and by what methods they should be made. It is not enough for the SITF to identify changes which would be "needed," because it is probable that these would be so numerous as to challenge the corporation's ability to carry them out. The SITF must establish priorities for its changes in a schedule for carrying them out. Further, because it is in a position to know, the SITF should generally specify the means by which the changes are to be implemented.

AN OVERALL PERSPECTIVE ON CHANGES TO BE RECOMMENDED

During the course of the concept audit the SITF will have identified changes of four basic types that it wishes to recommend. Three that were mentioned in the first chapter are:

1. The development of new or changes concepts.
2. The design of systems to implement accepted concepts.
3. The changing of actual operations or practices to conform with accepted concepts or systems.

The fourth, now mentioned for the first time, is change in strategy. As a practical matter, the process of conducting the concept audit is bound to reveal strategies so difficult to implement as to require momentous change. Also, in its general examination of conceptual design, the SITF is quite likely to uncover areas where strategy is needed but has not been adopted because of oversight. Such areas should, of course, be covered thoroughly when the SITF is reporting to top management.

In establishing priorities for change and the rate of action to be recommended, the SITF must look in two directions. First of all it must maintain sufficiently close contact with top management to know what management is willing to do about changing the company. Top management has final responsibility for changes, and no matter how logically and eloquently the SITF may argue for or against a new or changed conceptual approach, top management may reject some of its recommendations. The SITF's results depend upon how much meaningful change it accomplishes, not upon whether its recommendations are accepted in total.

If changes in concepts are dependent on top management attitudes, changes brought about by implementing concepts depend on the skills of the agent behind such change. At this point it should become clear to the SITF that the concept audit itself has been an instrument of change–usually in the attitudes of the members themselves as they realize that *they are now the key change agents of the corporation.* There are several reasons why the members of the SITF are uniquely qualified to implement design changes. If they were properly chosen for membership on the SITF, they are already in positions of leadership and influence throughout the company. Second, they should now have an in-depth understanding of the conceptual design of the company and its operation, including a view of the underlying need for change. And, finally, the SITF is in the intermediate position between top management and the operating levels of the company which carry out the concepts of top management. The SITF is in a sense the interpreter of the concepts of top management for those who are to carry them out through system design or implementation.

The SITF may specify a number of means for carrying out the recommended changes. One of the most effective vehicles is a temporary problem-solving task force. Unlike decision-making, problem-solving is an appropriate function of assigned group activity. It is especially appropriate when a large, complex program is involved, such as the detailed design of a system that has been conceptually spelled out by top management. In using such task forces, however, it is necessary to spell out carefully their responsibility and authority, to monitor their progress, and to end their existence when their work is over. Another means of implementing changes is to assign the responsibility to a specific executive who has authority over the area involved. Finally, the SITF should consider the need for specialized knowledge during the implementation phase. The emphasis in this book has been on the need for clear conceptual thinking. At some point in implementation, however, the technical specialist will probably be required. In planning for implementation, the SITF should make sure that such specialized knowledge will be brought to bear to the extent necessary.

CONCLUSIONS

The concept audit starts with a careful examination of the corporation's critical factors and related strategies. It proceeds to examine the concepts with which these strategies are executed in the design of the organization structure, management, management compensation, management and allocation of resources, and finally of the total corporation. The SITF may also decide to examine associated functional concepts along the way. When it has finished, it will have achieved the most comprehensive view possible of the corporation's fitness for meeting its objectives. When the program is complete, the SITF will also have produced an action plan by which important changes in the corporate design can be made. The new shape this gives the corporation can make the difference between a mediocre and a superior organization.

Appendix

Concept audit questions

GENERAL

Is there a general understanding of the economic concepts operating within the company, including the behavior of costs, the derivation of profits, and the flow of assets?

What are the important systems of the company, and are they recognized and treated as systems?

What is the operative level of understanding concerning the trends and development of the company and to what degree is it translated into specific plans and strategies?

What are the critical resources of the company and what conceptual basis is used to improve their productivity?

What kind of climate exists to support management vitality within the company and what kind is needed?

What specific things are intended to be accomplished by and through the organization structure?

What specific things are intended to be accomplished by and through the compensation system?

What are the typical approaches taken to improve the functioning of the corporation?

What changes have been identified as being needed in the design of the corporation?

ORGANIZATION STRUCTURE

What behavior should be defined by the organization structure?

What behavior is taking place outside of or in contradiction to the organization structure?

Does the organization structure define how individual units are related to each other?

Does the structure define how individual units are related to the overall mission of the corporation?

Is the definition of the organization structure sufficiently complete to reduce the need for direction from top management to a minimum?

Do managers make a disciplined effort to act according to the organization structure?

Is it necessary for managers to act in contradiction to the organization structure in order to be effective?

Does the organization structure cause tension among managers?

How much structure is appropriate for this organization?

What circumstances in this company indicate the need for an increase rather than a decrease in structure: fixed assets, internal efficiency, technology, managerial preference, the need to fix the response to events which may occur?

What are the special needs for coordination?

What means should be used to achieve coordination?

Which departments have a special need to cooperate?

Which departments have opportunities for conflict?

Is the structure designed to make real accountability possible?

Can results be traced to specific individuals?

Do managers have sufficient authority to influence the results for which they are held accountable?

Is the decision-making process designed so that the quality of decisions made can be improved?

Have committees been designed into the decision-making process appropriately?

Are committees making decisions that should be made by individuals who, unlike groups, can be held accountable for results?

What organizational relationship should be established between production and marketing?

What subfunctions within marketing and production require special organizational placement in order to receive appropriate emphasis or attention?

What are the most critical needs for coordination among the subfunctions in marketing and production?

What is the company committed to marketing?

To what basic type of production process is the company committed?

What production characteristics are significant in their influence on the marketing function?

Has the organization been designed to make the most effective use of the talents available?

Should specific responsibilities be increased or decreased to be in accord with the ability of the incumbent?

Is personal influence being used constructively and within the organizational structure?

Is the opportunity to exert influence without corresponding accountability being exercised with adequate responsibility?

Are groups of positions with close interactions designed holistically so as to take into account the combined talents of all of the executives involved?

Which functions need to be coordinated? What means should be used to achieve coordination?

MANAGEMENT

What corporate strategies are dependent upon management style and management qualities?

What are the corporate attitudes that must be reflected in manager attitudes?

Are managers receptive to and interested in change?

Is there a special requirement for risk takers, specialized professionals, or other recognizable types of managers?

How well are manager capabilities matched with position requirements?

Is the need for conceptualizing skill recognized adequately at each management level?

Are experience specifications stated in terms of time or in terms of meaningful exposure?

What basic manager attitudes are required for key positions?

What management style will create the attitudes and produce the performance critical to this company?

How democratic can the organization be?

Have the decisions which can be group decisions been carefully identified?

How should managers communicate with employees regarding performance?

What is the minimum satisfactory level of performance?

What should the manager do when performance standards are not met?

Is there an effective means for allowing managers to establish their own specific goals?

Is the goal-setting procedure such that managers become truly committed to the achievement of their goals?

Are individual manager goals aptly tied in with corporate goals?

Are performance reviews fully utilized for developmental and motivational purposes?

MANAGEMENT COMPENSATION

What are the overall goals of the compensation plan?

What corporate strategies should the compensation plan support?

What values are established by the compensation plan?

How generous should the fringe benefit package be?

What problems will be caused by omission of a pension plan?

Are stock options needed to attract and/or keep managers?

What kind of managers does the company wish to attract?

How high should the salary level be to attract managers?

At what level can the company afford to place salaries?

What effect, if any, should a bonus or incentive plan have on base salaries?

Do incentive programs justify lower base salaries?

Is compensation properly used as a response to performance?

Should response to performance be related to results or to the manager's performance and development?

How should salary increases be matched with performance?

RESOURCE ALLOCATION AND MANAGEMENT

Do managers manage operations instead of resources?

Are managers willing to eliminate inefficient resource users?

What resources limit the corporation's achievement of its goals?

Have all resource users been identified?

Has the productivity of resource users been measured?

Has direct profit contribution been established on a stand-alone basis for each profit source?

Is the behavior of each cost understood in relation to profit sources?

Is resource velocity maximized?

Is pricing policy geared to resource productivity?

Are the company's profit sources understood and treated as a total structure?

How much information on profit contribution and resource productivity is needed?

TOTAL CORPORATION

What is the corporate posture on the new forces at work in its environment?

Has this position been assumed on the basis of an honest consideration of the factors involved?

What is the appropriate measure of the corporation's performance?

Has responsibility for corporate design been assigned and accepted?

Have major corporate-wide systems been identified and dealt with as systems?

Have systems engineering approaches been used to improve corporate-wide systems?

Is the corporation keeping up with the development of knowledge?

Is the corporation using the latest management methods and tools to its advantage?

Does the corporation conduct research to improve its knowledge about its own functioning?

Are the performance standards being set from a total corporate point of view?

What is the nature of the changes that the corporation should make?

How rapidly should these changes be made?

Through what instruments or by what methods should the changes be made?

Index

This book is set in 11 and 10 point Press Roman, leaded 2 points. Chapter numbers are in 36 point Scotch Roman and chapter titles are in 24 point Scotch Roman italic. The size of the type page is 27 x 45 picas.